H I S T O R Y : Written and Lived

Other Publications of Paul Weiss

BOOKS

The Nature of Systems
Reality
Nature and Man
Man's Freedom
Modes of Being
Our Public Life
The World of Art
Nine Basic Arts

WITH OTHERS

American Philosophy Today and Tomorrow
Science, Philosophy, and Religion
Moral Principles of Action
American Philosophers at Work
Dimensions of Mind, etc.

EDITOR, WITH *Charles Hartshorne*

Collected Papers of Charles Sanders Peirce
   (SIX VOLUMES)

HISTORY:

Written and Lived

PAUL WEISS

SOUTHERN ILLINOIS UNIVERSITY PRESS

CARBONDALE

To Etienne Gilson

A GREAT HISTORIAN AND
A GREAT TEACHER.

PREFACE

A MULTILITHED VERSION of this book was sent to a number of interested friends, philosophers and historians, and was used by me in an undergraduate and in a graduate course. Richard J. Bernstein, Irwin C. Lieb, and Richard Sewall have kindly given me the benefit of their perceptive comments; Ellen S. Haring, Leonard Krieger, and Jonathan Weiss have made acute observations, criticisms and recommendations on almost every page and issue. I am grateful to all of them for their help, and wish only that I were able to do justice to all their doubts, difficulties, objections and suggestions.

This book is another testimony to my conviction that philosophy ought to be carried out on two levels. It should have a speculative dimension, where the whole of being and knowledge is in principle dealt with systematically by a distinctive method and in a distinctive style. This, my *Modes of Being* (1958) was intended to provide. There should also be an empirically oriented set of studies revealing the experienceable significance of the realities which the systematic study isolated. The present book is one of eight independent works devoted to this last endeavor. I have already dealt with the way in which men privately and publicly interplay with Actuality (*Reality*—1938—and *Nature and Man*—1947) and with the Ideal (*Man's Freedom*—1950—and *Our Public Life* —1959), and the way in which he privately takes account of Existence (*The World of Art*—1961—and *Nine Basic Arts*—1961). The present work is concerned with man's public use of Existence. It is to be followed by a study of his private and public involvement with the Divine. In each of these works different regions and disciplines are dealt with as autonomous domains, each with its own characteristic value, rationale, divisions and rhythms. Only such an effort, I think, avoids the temptation to reduce a basic enterprise or field to others, or to treat it merely as a variant or expression of them.

Very few philosophic attempts have been made to study a number of different fields in their own terms. Neglect of this fact has been particularly unfortunate for our present topic. The philosophy of history is a comparatively new subject. Men have therefore been inclined to deal with it in terms of established categories, disciplines and methods valuable in other areas, and have as a consequence tended to reduce it to an aspect or variant of older but quite different studies. When sensitive to the particular problems raised by the philosophy of history, they have usually been content to introduce new categories and make some new distinctions. But this procedure, too, supposes that the older ideas are relevant to this new subject. I have found, as a rule, that justice cannot be done to the nature of history except by taking a fresher, more sympathetic approach to it than is customarily the case. The accident of the late arrival of the study of the philosophy of history ought not to be allowed to preclude a philosophic consideration of history in the same spirit as that which now characterizes older disciplines. And that means, I think, that its categories and problems must be treated organically, as modifying and supplementing one another.

One of the claims of the present work is that it takes history seriously, as a domain with a distinctive being and rationale. The price paid is that much remains obscure and confused, a good deal sounds paradoxical, and some of it surely will not be able to withstand the criticism I hope it will receive.

PAUL WEISS

New Haven, March, 1962.

CONTENTS

H I S T O R Y : Written and Lived

INTRODUCTION

MEN HAVE DRAWN many conclusions from history. Few of these conclusions have won a large measure of agreement from historians or from other men. History is evidently a difficult subject to master or profit from. And philosophy appears to be at least as recalcitrant a subject as history; indeed, philosophers seem to have profited less from a study of philosophy than historians have from history.

Since "philosophy of history" sounds as if it were an amalgam of history and philosophy, it would seem to be a more difficult subject than either pure philosophy or history. Actually, a philosophy of history is no more difficult than either; it is in fact more capable than either of yielding knowledge and conviction, for though less searching it is more empirical than pure philosophy, and though not as detailed or concrete it is more systematic than history.

A philosophy of history does not offer a fullblown philosophy. It does not concern itself with the "last" questions—the nature of those ultimate conditions and realities in terms of which all knowledge and being are to be understood. Since its range is not as wide and the beings of which it speaks are not as recondite as those dealt with in a pure philosophy, its claims can be tested more readily than philosophy's. Its results too can be more intelligible than history's, since they are expressible in terms of abstract reasons, principles and categories, and not in terms of concrete causes, outcomes and the relations between these. There need in fact be about as much history in it as there is lobster in lobster sauce. The limitations of history—and of course its achievements—ought not to be confused with those characteristic of a philosophy of history.

A philosophy of history is a distinctive inquiry, with its own methods, rationale, criteria and achievements. One of its objectives is to understand what historians ideally do and accomplish. It inquires into the historian's motives and methods, examines his distinctive questions and problems, and tries to determine the value of his work. It also seeks to provide an account of the world about which the historian discourses. This must be done if we are to be able to know whether or not there is anything else to be learned about the historic world than what the historian reports. No other enterprise than the philosophy of history has these as its primary topics. From no other therefore can we hope to understand what the historian can know, how his discipline differs from others, whether or not the historic world can be adequately dealt with by him, and how that world is related to nature and whatever other realms and realities there might be. Only the philosophy of history faces up to such questions as: How can we inquire into the past? Why should we? How can we tell whether or not we are speaking truly or falsely regarding it? Must history be constantly rewritten? How long is the historic present? Are there historic laws? Is everything that has happened part of history? Does the historic world have its own distinctive time, space, power, causation? How is it possible for a man to be both an historic and a natural being?

Our discussion readily divides into two parts. The first begins by attending to the similarities and differences between history and science. It then moves on to deal with the problems which are raised by any attempt to know the past and to communicate what one knows. The second part deals with the world which the historian presupposes. It points up the fact that that world has a being, a structure and a career different from that possessed by any other.

The historian, I will argue, can truly know the historic past. And no one else can know what items it contains. If we are to find out what has happened, we must therefore inquire and conclude with historians. But the past has a being which the historian takes for granted and which cannot be fully grasped by following his methods. To understand it we must speculate. We will then become aware not only of the fact that the historic world is sustained by and exhibits powers which are nonhistoric in origin, but that it is part of a larger world. The realities on which the historian reports are sustained by nonhistoric powers. These are primarily in various individuals, or groups of them and in nature, i.e. that portion of cosmic Existence which is relevant to man's public career. The historic world encompasses an ordered sequence of occurrences in which groups of men, or their representatives, publicly take account of the presence or action of some of nature's powers. It is an accumulative world, one in which what has happened is related to and kept in relation with what follows after. Ceremonies, rituals, traditions, and above all the controlled guidance of an end, makes it possible for men not only to act publicly but, with the concurrence of nature, to constitute and be part of an objective history.

To have an historic world, mankind or its representatives must publicly act in a distinctive time, on nature or its representatives. The swirling sand in the lonely desert is time-bound; but since it has as yet no place in human affairs it is not part of the historic world. The pain I feel is also temporal; but so long as I suffer it in silence it is too private to be part of the historic world. When I speak to my children my words are public, but they are the words of an individual addressed to individuals. I could represent the larger world to my children as a diplomat might represent his nation, but we still would not be part of an historic world unless we together then became part of a single sequential order, embracing all men.

A society, institution, state, nation, mob, horde, or populace is a public group which publicly interacts with various powers. Sometimes those powers are located in other groups, at other times they are to be found in individuals; they are always exhibited in nature as it stands over against all men. If the groups are held apart from mankind, and if there is no accumulative order to the interlocked activities of the various groups and nature, no historic world is produced.

The historic world is the world of objective history; the narrative of this is history, *tout court*. The two, the historic and history, objective history and its investigation and narrative, are frequently confounded. But they are so distinct that one can forge an apparent self-contradiction merely by speaking of both at the same time and not using different terms for them: History is not history. The contradiction dissolves with the recognition that "history" is here being used to refer both to what has happened and to an account of what has happened. The two are distinct in being and in career, though they may occasionally coincide in fact. Coincident or not, they are produced in different ways, and are subject to different evaluations now and later. The one is produced by public men, covers large areas and is primarily past; the other is produced by private men in a limited part of the present as the outcome of a critical inquiry and a disciplined adventure in imagination and construction. The one is rarely the product of deliberation and will; the other is usually so.

A history may of course have historic import; it can be given a public role and be made part of an historic occurrence. It can then become the topic of some other written history. As written about, the first history will then have two roles; it will offer an historical account of something historic, and it will be part of an historic occurrence to which the second history refers.

Though we rarely have reliable knowledge of historic occurrences unless we engage in history, it is nevertheless true that not every historic occurrence finds a place in a history; inquiry may not have yet, and perhaps may never alight on some past item. A history refers to historic occurrences distinct from it in availability, nature, condition and cause. This truth seems to be rejected by Croce, Ortega y Gasset and apparently also by Collingwood. These men deny that a history makes reference to an objective, past, historic world. But if they were right, there would be nothing to which a history would be said to refer. A history would then be indistinguishable from an idle fancy, a sheer fiction.

In contrast, the followers of Ranke—though not he —think that a history mirrors the historic. In effect they deny that history requires interpretation, reorganization, selection, analysis, and the adoption of a perspective which is never final. They seem to forget that history is an intellectual enterprise, subject to the conditions and limitations which beset all inquiry. After all, a history can tell us what happened only if it translates its evidences and conclusions into hypotheses and narrations. It can tell us what is truly the case only if it refuses to describe or to chronicle, and instead reassesses, fills out, explains, reconstructs and interprets. To be most precise, to be most accurate, to say exactly what is the case, one must dress up the naked facts on which inquiry alights. They must be given a context, neighbors, powers, and related to inferred antecedents and possible consequences.

Both the Croceans and the Rankians fail to do full justice to many recordings which are part of the historic world. The Croceans tend to speak of monuments, documents, and histories as though they were ideas, to be used in some subsequent history; the others tend to turn them into nothing but historic occurrences, failing to see that they are also legitimate reports of what happened. The first do not see that a monument can ground, test and pivot the account of it in some history; the others do not see that a monument can offer a true or false record of some more remote part of objective history. In contrast with both we ought to say, I think, that monuments and the like are not ideas, not necessarily part of recorded history, nor mere occurrences in an endless continuum. They are pivotal historic points. Since they can ground strong inferences to important preceding states of affairs, they can and ought to offer pivotal points for a written history. They are moreover to be used, as we shall see, in exactly the way other historic evidence is to be used. A monument, a document, or a ruin usually differs from other pieces of historic evidence only in being more conspicuous, more important, more interesting, or more readily available.

Both the Croceans and the Rankians flatten out

the historic world; they ignore the fact that there are sharp turns, closures and stresses within it. Since every historian periodizes his material, he would, if there were no pivotal points in the historic world, be engaged in the arbitrary subdivision of a single continuum of occurrences. Fortunately, historians are never forced to be that high-handed. They know that a ruin marks the end of one historic process, a monument another, a document a third, a war a fourth, a peace treaty a fifth, a revolution, an alliance, an invention, a discovery still others. For each one of these there is a relevant beginning from which an historical narrative could take its start.

Historians also know that the present is the end of whatever past there is. This is true even when nothing of importance is happening in that present. The point is obvious, constantly misunderstood or overlooked—and of enormous importance. The historian quite clearly begins with something present. He could not avoid doing so. All his data are to be found there. He can perceive, observe, and think in no other time than the present.

Because the present is the end of whatever past there be, and because it may be a present in which nothing of importance is happening, we tend to misconstrue the past and to suppose that all of it is equally relevant, that it is a single mass of items all on a footing. But though nothing of consequence may be happening in the present, some items there always stand out over against others, for the historian, warranting a search for their antecedents. The present is the end of a past, and in that past and in the present there are in fact and for the historian peaks and valleys, cut-off points, relevant beginnings for distinguished endings.

The historian writes as though his mind were

geared to an order in which cause was followed by effect; but he actually proceeds by beginning with effects and ending his inquiry with the discovery of their causes. Because we usually come to know of the historian's work through the narrative that he provides, and since this proceeds in a chronological order, from a more remote to a less remote past, we tend to overlook the fact that at least half of his work is devoted to the determination of relevant causes for accepted outcomes. The past on which he focuses is important because it is relevant to the end with which he began his inquiry. The items to which he infers are not merely conditions for the items he isolates in the present; by virtue of their relation to present items, they have a status different from what they had when they were present.

The historian is teleologically minded, one who looks at the past as defined in part by what comes later. And his attitude partly answers to the constitution of the historic world. Like the historian's inquiry, the historic world—as will become more evident in the course of this work—is governed by a final cause giving a value, direction and meaning to what precedes it. But where the historian necessarily begins in a present (itself passing away), in which he focuses on a number of objects and occurrences, the historic world is governed by a permanent and inclusive end which enables every occurrence relevant to mankind's career to have an historic role. The historian thinks teleologically before he writes chronologically; the historic is governed teleologically when and as it becomes chronologically. Because the teleological movement in both cases has often been overlooked or minimized, it is desirable to attend to the fact for a while.

The attitudes of historians is a function of unexamined experiences and interests. Though one historian's attitude differs in detail from another's, and may be different in important respects at different times, there is a permanent core to be discerned in all of them, reflecting the historians' concern for certain pivotal occurrences and values. All historians, e.g., are alert to the importance of birth, marriage, death, to the difference in pace that is characteristic of the periods of youth, maturity and old age, to the centrality of such occurrences as peace, war, prosperity, crises, competition, power, wealth and poverty. All know that men fear and hope, that they are never wholly good or wholly bad, that they are governed by multiple motives, and that they are at once selfish and altruistic, sensible and foolish, and at unpredictable times. And they have some knowledge of what slows up communication, what breeds distrust, what supports power. The historian is a reasonable man armed with the wisdom and knowledge possessed by other mature men in his society. Most important, he looks at what happened not only as a condition, but as present in, accumulated by, and operative on what follows it.

The historian's attitude enables him to convert what would otherwise be an external departed occurrence into an historical one, linked to some successor in accordance with what reasonable men take to be plausible ways. Since our idea of the reasonable is in good part a function of social experiences, all histories have a tribal side, reflecting the assumptions and evaluations shared by the members of a society. There is no need, however, to lament this fact. It serves to remind us that a history cannot be presumed to be more reasonable than an historian can be. The historian, when dealing with a people or a time other than his own, adjusts his attitudes, alters his interpretations of what it would then be reasonable to expect; if he did not, he would be provincial, irrational, unwilling to allow for the different needs, affiliations, tasks, stresses and values which characterize those other times. A history too may be more rational, accurate and precise than any historian can be, since it is partly the cooperative product of a disciplined inquiry making use of evidence and logic, and minimizing any one historian's bias and excess by confronting these with opposing biases and excesses, and some indubitable facts.

In addition to a distinctive attitude, the historian has an outlook which enables him to see the past as embracing an ordered and directed set of historical occurrences. The evidence which he uses helps him to isolate particular items in the past as the relevant antecedents of that evidence. Since the historian is constantly discovering new evidence, he is constantly forced to re-evaluate what he or others had previously judged to be important or unimportant. Were it not for the fact that the changes required by such new evidence is usually slight, he would be forced to write a new history every day. Still, new evidence does sometimes help him see that what he thought was of no historical value actually has considerable importance.

The historian's awareness of the objective reality of various historic items, not relevant to his present evidence, enables him to re-estimate what he had already taken to be historic. Historians accumulate many facts for which they have no apparent use or place, dimly aware that they are historic facts that may eventually turn out to be relevant to some new inquiry. Were it not for the fact that the historian is aware that newly acknowledged items were parts of an objective history, he would have to say that he had converted those items from occurrences in nature or society into occurrences in history. But then his history would be neither true nor false.

Relations in the objective historic world run, as was observed before, in two directions: from past to present and future, and from future and present to past. If either type of relation is held apart from the other, some historic occurrences will be passed over, and the rest will be misunderstood. The terminus of the forward movement is an *outcome*. Whatever happens—in the moments still to come, in the moment in which we now are, and in the moments that have been—are all outcomes. No one of these outcomes need to be aimed at. Nor need it be superior in value or importance to any other kind of occurrence or to what might have occurred instead. And it ought not to be treated as absolutely final, since if it were, whatever happened after it would have to be viewed as nonhistoric. No outcome is unquestionably final; at no one moment can we say that the historic world has come to an end.

The present defines all that is in a direct causal line to it to be *effective* for it. Since this present gives way to others and since, also, many things occur which are not relevant to one present or another, or even to all subsequent presents, and since some public human activities are futile or have had their efficacy exhausted in the past, the historic world defined by a present outcome evidently includes but part of what ought to be recognized as historic.

He who promoted the occurrence of some achieved outcome is so far effective. If his outcome is effective with respect to some later one, he is also mediately effective. But if his outcome is not effective with respect to some later one, he is, from the standpoint of that later outcome, without historic causal *significance*. His effectiveness would have had only a limited span, inside of which he had an historic role. Since he is not mediately effective with respect to the outcome at which the historic world subsequently arrives, it is as if, at that time, he and his works never had been. As a matter of fact he does have a place in objective history which he never loses, but this one can know and affirm only by taking account of more than outcomes.

Men of action, politicians, generals, kings and the like are always effective for some limited span. If they fail to reach the goals they set themselves, they are maladroit, incompetent. As men of action, however, as men who represent or lead others, they are always effective for a time, causally significant, since they then interact with external forces in such a way as to bring about historic outcomes. But even if they attain the goals they set themselves, they may not have historic significance in terms of some later outcome.

It is the faith of many men of action that theirs is always a causally significant life, particularly when they succeed in bringing about the goals they set themselves. They are mistaken. They may have spent their energies producing what is without subsequent historic issue. This seems to be true of the kings of ancient Sumeria. And it seems to be true of many who are alive and important today. Britain, after the second world war, entered a new period in which new forces operated to promote the dissolution of the empire. The preceding period was dominated by Churchill's masterly leadership in the war and his activities on behalf of the empire. The victory he helped bring about terminated that period and put a limit to the effectiveness of his idea of the empire. The Churchill who led his nation in war remains of significance today because he is mediately effective with reference to the peace that Britain now enjoys. But the Churchill of the empire has little significance today, and it seems most likely that it will not be long before he has none at all.

The occurrences in history are not only linked in a relation running from past to future; they are governed by a relation which moves from future to past. The fact becomes obvious when we reflect on the truth that no outcome is ever entirely as it ought to be. At every moment there is much that is regrettable. What has been achieved over the course of history is not yet what ought to have been achieved.

The historic *ought-to-be* is to be sharply distinguished from what an historian and his contemporaries may take to be excellent, worthwhile, right. All of us tend to read and often to rewrite history in terms of the values cherished only at our later time. We tend today to denigrate Greece because it had slaves and to praise it because it had a scientific temper; we are inclined to dismiss or to honor the theologians of the middle ages in the light of our estimate of the value of religion. Though we in these ways show a possibly commendable loyalty to the values accepted by our group, we in fact reveal ourselves to be provincial, exhibiting the very antithesis of the spirit which should animate the historian.

One should try to enter into a period with an awareness of what might have been achieved there. Only he who takes such an approach will be able to do full justice to its promise, and therefore to take proper account of its blunders and successes. Though this approach is at the other extreme from that adopted by the provincially-minded, it is, if alone pursued, no more satisfactory in the end than the other, for it confines us too much to a limited segment of history, and does not allow us to compare one type of outcome with another. We have no warrant for condemning Rome because it did not produce great philosophers; its structure, drives, aspirations and opportunities led it elsewhere. But this need not prevent us from judging its culture to be less advanced than ours or the Greeks'. The historic ought-to-be is thus to be sharply distinguished from what would be a fitting end to some particular historic period.

The historic ought-to-be is not the absolute good. Such a good has a bearing on ethical decisions, on men in their privacy; it relates to subhumans as well as to humans; it has too wide a range to be pertinent only to history. The historic ought-to-be, since it refers to a plurality of men interplaying with external forces, is at best only a delimited form of this absolute good.

Many of those who have pledged themselves to a life of religion, or who have followed the lead of Hegel's philosophy of history, have adopted the view that the historic ought-to-be is a predestined outcome. Persuaded that the historic world will eventually arrive at the stage where it ought-to-be—when history and its time apparently will come to an end—they try to make it dominate their outlook. Since the end is taken by them to be inescapable, it is unnecessary for them to act on behalf of it. When they urge others to act in certain ways they can, on this view, only be prodding those others merely to take a place inside the only frame where they can be historic beings.

The man of action rightly chides the believers in such an historic ought-to-be for making unwarranted assumptions. He remarks that believers in an historic ought-to-be have not made its nature clear, that they have no way of knowing that it will be realized, and that if it is taken to be predestined many effective human plans, creations, achievements will be denied an historic place. Most important, a mere ought-to-be, predestined or not, he sees, is too selective if it operates in abstraction from everything that men actually do in public in interaction with external forces. In response, the believers in an ought-to-be attack the man of action as amoral and foolish, since he ignores the reality of values and the possibility that effective work in the present may have no historic significance. Each side wrongly rejects what the other affirms, and each exaggerates what it itself discerns. The one wrongly supposes that the ought-to-be will surely come about as an outcome of an historic process, and the other wrongly supposes that what is now effective will surely be significant. Neither is able to say, as one should, that all men have produced in public through an interplay with exterior forces is historic, that different items in the historic world have different values measurable by one ought-to-be, and that this ought-to-be can govern the past only by going through the gateway of the present.

An historic ought-to-be which had to be arrived at could now be only a possible outcome, at once inevitable and good. Though it would make possible the evaluation of whatever happened, as being good or bad, it would preclude the occurrence of genuine historic contingencies, novelties, accidents, and make it incorrect to say that the future is a function of what happens in the present, incorrect to say that at every moment history arrives at an outcome for which preceding occurrences are effective, and incorrect to say that the whole of history can be less good than it could have been. It is a mistake therefore to treat the historic ought-to-be as an outcome with which the historic *must* come to an end.

The present allows some past occurrences to have historic significance—those which are effective with respect to it. The historic ought-to-be gives an historic role both to those items and to others as well, because it evaluates them all as items having some relation to the present, itself evaluated as more or less desirable. By operating through the present the historic ought-to-be is able to assess whatever is significant for that present as being instrumentally good or bad, and to assess whatever is not significant for that present as being a desirable or undesirable hindrance to the production of that present. What, from the standpoint of a present outcome may be without significance is thus, through the operation of the historic ought-to-be, given historic status.

Much happens during a war that is not germane to the outcome; from the standpoint of the outcome these occurrences are without historic significance. But nothing escapes the historic ought-to-be. What is without historic significance is endowed by it with the historic status of being a desirable or undesirable hindrance, slowing up the pace of historic time. If we eliminate all hindrances, the effective line from beginning to end of the war will be as it was. But then the historic time of the war will no longer have to move through and around the hindrances which the complete historic war includes. The time of that war will consequently be different from what it in fact had been.

The historic ought-to-be encompasses all history. It demands that men be one, not be broken up into factions, not be opposed to one another's presence, being or promise. It obligates men to live in peace. Since men are divided not only against themselves but against the world outside, it makes it a duty of men that they become adjusted to the world—that, in short, they prosper. And since men are not merely bodies, but have minds and wills, it demands that they be able to engage in the crafts, arts, science, and commerce, to develop their personalities, and to practice virtue. The historic ought-to-be asks of objective history that public men, severally and together, be there fulfilled, be at their best. Every outcome is defective to the degree it falls short of this historic ideal. Whatever is ineffective with respect to such a defective outcome is a desirable hindrance, slowing up the historic time by which that defective outcome was attained.

The historian should take at least some account of the reality of the historic ideal, for this guarantees that items, which are not known to be significant for him or for his present, nevertheless have an historic role, affecting the time and perhaps the import of the historic realities that he knows. It enables him to pass an unbiased judgment on the villainies and follies, the heroisms and achievements of the past, and to evaluate the perspective which he in the present takes with reference to what had been. So far as he takes account of the ought-to-be that governs the course of history, he knows there are items in the historic past that are relevant to, though not significant for the present. That past can have a being over against him only if there is a power which can keep the past in being, despite the fact that it has passed away. The historian should take account of this power too, if he wishes to know how an historic world can be, and how it can make it possible for him to say what is true or false. The work of an historian, however, does not require him, strictly speaking, to make explicit reference to that power or even to the historic ought-to-be.

I

THE

RECOVERY OF THE PAST

I

History and Science

A PHILOSOPHIC STUDY of history today finds a great
obstacle athwart its path in the shape of a belief that
science and history cannot both be basic disciplines,
telling us, through the use of distinctive techniques
and procedures, what in fact is true. Most men today
would insist that history should either assume the
form of a science or admit that it is nothing but a
tissue of guesses and opinions. Their outlook is still
somewhat like that which Descartes so forcefully and
persuasively presented three hundred years ago. They
agree with him in thinking that we come closest to
doing justice to the nature of the real by following
the methods or by accepting the conclusions of
mathematics and the mathematical sciences. Any aspect of the universe or any discipline which requires
a different set of concepts from those appropriate to a
scientifically known world will, from this point of
view, be treated as illusory in whole or part, and will

therefore be dismissed, reduced to mathematics, or revealed to be based on a confusion in supposition, method or language. The concrete particularity of history's events, its novelties, its unamenability to pure deductive and a priori procedures, its involvement with process and events, its concern with time's asymmetry, and its interest in what has passed away seem to many to warrant one of these fates.

Some thinkers, particularly Vico, Croce and Collingwood, clearly see the unwarranted nature of the common assumption that only what is reported in mathematics or science is ultimate, and irreducibly true. But they then go on to commit the same error as their opponents do, though from the opposite side. Instead of taking mathematics or science to report the nature of the real, they suppose that history does, and that what does not really fit into an historic scheme is necessarily illusory, derivative, or confused. But mathematics, logic and science are surely no less legitimate, ultimate or truthful than history. The assassination of Lincoln was more than a matter of ballistics and the transition of a man from life to death; it was an historic event having its own rhythm and rationale. It was unique, irreducible, with peculiar antecedents and consequences. But the bullet flew in accord with the laws of ballistics, and the life of Lincoln ebbed in ways which doctors and biologists could predict. No view is adequate which does not allow us to say that it is true that Lincoln was assassinated, and also true to say that he died, and that the one assertion is neither a variation of nor reducible to the other.

History is distinct from science in subject matter, problem, procedure, test and outcome. Neither is occupied with brute realities or even with descriptions of these. Neither is a set of mere suppositions or a simple report of what is the case. Every science offers hypotheses, constructions, laws, whose function it is to enable one to understand the nature, interrelationship and occurrence of phenomena; every history attends to the available evidence and subjects its interpretations to criticisms and tests which are rigorous and reliable. The subject matter of both is what is the case. But science attempts to understand it through the use of elements whose interplay can be portrayed in a formal account, whereas history seeks to understand it by tracing the process by which it came about.

There is a stress in science on the repeatable features of things, and a stress in history on what has occurred and can occur only once. From this we should not conclude that science is concerned solely with laws and that history is concerned only with singular events. Science sometimes attends to the singular; it occupies itself with such unrepeatable occurrences as the explosion of a nova or the evolution of some now defunct species. And there can be a history of laws of nature, particularly if, as Peirce held, they are subject to evolution. Nor should we conclude that the assertions of science are all eternal truths expressed in terms of variables capable of receiving many different values, and that the assertions of history are transitory or contingent claims expressed by means of constants having only one application. Some assertions of geology, botany or astronomy are conspicuously oriented towards a definite region of space and time, and take account of singular experiments or experiences. Historians sometimes offer laws or state necessities which all occurrences are thought to exemplify; and they always take some account of the laws of human thinking, behavior and social activity. Both science and history take for granted laws discovered or supposed in other disciplines; both attend to phenomena not altogether articulatable in laws. The enterprise of history has a scientific aspect, involving as it does instruments, men and energy; science, since it is a product of human activity, accumulative, directed, causative over time, has an historical side. Every item in history can be made the object of a scientific study; every achievement of science has a place in objective history and can have one in a written history. The disciplines nevertheless are distinct.

The subject matter of science differs from that of history. To see this most clearly, let us take a conceivable case which might interest both disciplines and let us express it in a most simplified form. We are confronted, let us suppose, with organisms of a certain type, all of which at one time had a one-chambered heart and later a two-chambered one. A scientist would be interested in the difference between these two types of heart and would seek to determine the pattern of change through which the organisms went in response to altered conditions. An historian would be interested in the process connecting the junctures which the different hearts made with their different conditions. The one would attend to structures and would only incidentally note the particular hearts and their adventures; the other would attend to the process actually gone through by the hearts as interplaying with the world about, and would only incidentally note the structure of the process. A scientist might of course interest himself in the way in which the hearts reacted to different circumstances, but this would be because he had turned from the question of the origin of the two-chambered heart to a new question—that of the structure of the adjustments which had been made to the different environments. Were an historian to interest himself in the adjustments made to the different environments, he would note the various responses which in fact took place in a definite order and which finally terminated in the adjustment of the two-chambered hearts.

The subject matter for the scientist is the elements, laws or principles exemplified in the process of transformation, whereas for the historian the problem is to know what the actual process, as undergone by some particulars, was like. The one is concerned with a pattern which a process sustains, the other with a process which might exemplify a pattern. Faced with the same date they occupy themselves with quite different aspects of it. Science and history would be correlative disciplines were they both concerned with maintaining a grasp on the aspects which interest the other. But the historian turns as soon as he can from the structure to consider the actual process, whereas the scientist turns as soon as he can from the process to consider the structure. If the historian states a law he but rigidifies and generalizes a process. If a scientist assigns a date, it is one oriented towards an abstract, nontemporal present, a zero point of origin for a series of plus and minus numbers. (See *The World of Art*, Chapter 4, for a more extended treatment of this point.)

A second illustration, more perhaps to the liking of the historian, is presented by the difference between the Greeks and the Romans. Let us suppose this difference to consist solely in the fact that the Greeks had outstanding creative philosophers and that the Romans did not. Let us suppose that the absence of philosophers in the latter case was due to an increased interest in the law on the part of the Romans.

A scientist faced with these data would take as his subject matter the rationale of the connection between an interest in law and an absence of philosophers. He would attend to the process, which had in fact taken place, only so far as this enabled him to catch the structure of the connection. The historian, instead, would be concerned with knowing the process, with understanding the way in which the interest in law had brought about a loss of interest in creative philosophy. Both would attend to the process; both would attend to the pattern which was carried out in the process. But the one would seek to isolate the pattern and would eventually deal with this alone, whereas the other would seek to recover the process and in the end would submerge any known pattern within it.

So-called historical laws are really summary statements of processes; so-called scientific descriptions of processes are really static patterns assigned dates and places. The historian might be interested in discovering some such law as that which links an advance in technology with a defeat of a nation, the relation of the increase in democracy to literacy or freedom, the cyclical recurrence of changes in such fashions as the use of beards, canes, low waists, etc. But if he attends to these primarily as having a constant nature which happens to be carried out in this place or time, he speaks as a naturalistic scientist or reflective philosopher rather than as an historian. A scientist, conversely, might be interested in determining just when some event occurred, but if he thinks of this date as immersed in the context of a single temporal movement he speaks as an historian rather than as a scientist, even of the most "naturalistic" variety. The scientist tries to produce a rational, formal scheme, an intelligible account with determinate kinds of repeatable, analyzable, and if possible mathematically formulatable patterns; the historian seeks to know through just what steps an actual process proceeded. Where the historian wants to see how something got to where it now is from where it had been, the scientist wants to know what principles were operative in whatever process happened to take place.

Science and history not only have different subject matters, since the one concentrates on structures and the other on processes, but they also are occupied with different problems, due in part to the fact that they have different subject matters. Both face something in the present that sets them to wondering and inquiring, to questioning and reflecting. This can be some odd matter of fact, but with the development of the institutional nature of these disciplines, with their academic interests and periodicals, it often is not. In both disciplines, problems are frequently set by discrepancies in the reports or positions of other workers in the field. But no matter how set, what the scientist finds arresting the historian often does not, and conversely. The historian looks for or comes across something out of place, something in the present which cannot be understood by treating it alongside the other items where it is found. He wants to know how it came to be there, why the present has just the assemblage of items or shows just the features and distributions which it does. The scientist might see nothing amiss where the historian finds much to remark. What sets the scientist moving is the question of how objects which are diverse can be in the same universe, and he seeks to know the principles and elements in terms of which the diversity could be intellectually mastered.

The two take different attitudes, particularly in

modern times, towards common-sense data. For the scientist the things of everyday are not finally intelligible in everyday terms. They must be analyzed, reinterpreted, expressed in highly general and preferably mathematical forms. He finds that the only way in which he can predict the future of the state of affairs which he now confronts, in consonance with predictions made with respect to other objects at other times, is by turning away from the things as they appear or are commonly understood, and then occupying himself with the formulation of precise and universally applicable laws relating items which, by combination and interplay, could conceivably constitute what he confronts. He does not deny that there are desks and chairs, microscopes and scales; he knows he uses them, and that no theory, no matter how successful in promoting predictions, or how comprehensive, clear or rational, is warranted in terming them nonexistent. But he knows that there is little he can learn from them by attending to them in their daily forms. If he is to understand them and all else he must express what they are in terms of units which can conceivably compose other things, and must show how these units are interrelated in such a way that the subsequent careers of desks and chairs, microscopes and scales and the like can be understood and perhaps predicted. He can see, as everyone else does, that heavy bodies fall faster than light ones, but he turns his back on that empirically ascertainable truth to attend to the idea of atomic units falling in an absolute vacuum. Laws formulated for that ideal—perhaps even impossible—state of affairs enable him to deal with all types of fall so far as these can be inferred by making quantitative qualifications, alterations and additions in the ideal state of affairs. In the end he will accept what he observed in the beginning —e.g., that heavy bodies fall faster than light ones— but will explain the fact as involving the intersection and combination of laws governing an ideal state of affairs.

The historian, in contrast, never abandons common sense. For him heavy bodies fall faster than light ones. This does not mean that he is stupid, obstinate, ignorant or unteachable, but only that the historical world is one peopled with common-sense objects. Now, "common sense" has a number of senses. It refers to the conventional, familiar world of every day to which we have been trained to fit, a socially conditioned world which varies in content and meaning from place to place and time to time. It refers also to a nuclear meaning common to different societal common-sensical worlds. The nuclear common-sense world is the world known to engineers, fishermen, sailors—to all those who are experienced in the ways of the world. A third meaning of common sense refers to the objects of the moral and aesthetic sensitivity of men either in some period, in more than one society, or as making up one mankind. Judgments, values, and standards, though still socially determined, here refer to men and activities, some of which are outside one's own group; they allow one to judge the behavior of one's own group, not necessarily favorably. A fourth sense of the term has reference to a combination of the first three. It relates to the wisdom of a people, the kind of understanding which lawyers and judges, the older and more respected members of the community possess. The world of these men is partly conventional, partly nuclear and partly evaluative; at its best it focusses on what is at once socially sanctioned, practical, moral, and wise. A fifth meaning of common sense is whatever is naively experienced, accepted without reflection. This meaning is always in the background of the other four and grounds a continuity between the attitudes and activities of child and adult, the innocent and the disciplined.

All men act in terms of all five common-sensical outlooks. The historian's report of what men do and why they do it will therefore be in error if it does not take account of the fact that the men and their institutions have these outlooks as content, stimulus, and objective. The historian cannot of course avoid beginning his investigation with an acknowledgment of the familiar conventionalized world, but he must also attend to the nuclear, practical, moral and precognitive meanings, and use the result to test and measure the truth of conventionalized judgments. In the end he must locate the result inside a larger naively experienced world, to constitute a reliable outcome which is to be supplemented, supported and contrasted by what one might learn from science and religion, through speculation and art.

That heavy bodies fall faster than light ones is a nuclear truth. All men live and act in terms of it. The historian never rightly questions it. Though an assassination is not possible except where there are rulers and some law and order, though its impact is usually confined to some small segment of the globe and is causally effective for only a short period, the historian recognizes it too to be a brute fact open to the nuclear observational powers of any one who knows the structure of a given society. The historian however is also alert to the fact that the area in which objective history occurs, the kind of causation it exhibits, the way in which the past is accumulated and the way in which it is preserved are peculiar to it. Concerned as he is with knowing the past, he can do little more in the end than accept the five-fold common-sensical outlook as providing a setting for what had been.

Both the scientist and the historian ask, "why this?" The historian, though, wants to know why it came about, what caused it, where and when the cause occurred. He moves back into the past from a gross and obtrusive present, and there tries to recover the start of a signal series of equally gross occurrences. He knows that past items are not identical in nature or being with what they were when they were present. Past items, he recognizes, are fully determinate, merely factual; they are paralyzed realities, dessicated common-sense entities, interlocked with a dessicated part of nature.

The historian does not want to analyze either past or present items into elements which can be ordered by rational laws, making possible a cosmic system of formal and predictable knowledge. When he wants to know the where, when, why and how it is always with respect to macroscopic occurrences. If a scientist were to ask all the above questions they would mean for him quite different things from what they mean for the historian. "From what" means for the scientist the elements analyzable out of gross objects, or their causes; "where" and "when" refer to a dating inside a scientific calendar; "why" refers him to a reason not to a power, to a "because" rather than to a "cause"; and "how" relates him to operations and transformations conceived to be under the guidance of some rule, rather than to a process which in fact once occurred and was in principle open to gross observation.

The scientist's problems though are best expressed through the use of a different set of questions from those which have most pertinence to the historian.

What the scientist wants to know is what elements are constituents in all things; how they are rationally related to one another; how they can be understood to come together so as to present us with the objects of gross observation; what more general laws are illustrated by any local predictable set of occurrences; and how one can in principle transform one entity into any other. He seeks elements which can be described in formal terms alone, and whose interconnection will account for the diversity of the objects and occurrences we can daily note. He does not concern himself with the unrepeatable, vital movement of a process, but only with the rationale it might exhibit. Were the historian to ask the very same questions that the scientist does he would mean different things by them. In asking what the elements of a thing might be the scientist wants to get to the essence of the thing, whereas the historian wants to know the relevant antecedents for it. In asking how a thing is put together the scientist wants to know the rules or laws which are being exemplified, whereas the historian wants to know the actual course of events which had that result as outcome. In asking what makes an object observable the historian seeks to know what factors make what otherwise would be hidden into something open to public knowledge; in asking about general laws he asks after the repeatable guides that have had a role inside a given period; and in asking how one thing might be transformed into another he seeks to know the particular steps gone through by some actual transformation. The scientist's items could conceivably be in a reverse order, and some of the rules he isolates could conceivably apply to the items in that reverse order without altering the import of the rules or of the items. The historian does not, except incidentally, ever ask himself if the transformation could have been reversed, for the items with which he deals are for him in an irreversible order.

The procedures of the two disciplines are also distinct. Though both attend to evidence and engage in inference (sometimes reaching data and consequences considerably distant from the place in space or time where the inquirer is), and though both surmise, adventure, forge hypotheses, imagine, construct, they do so along quite different lines. The scientist tries to make his observations fit inside a frame which he accepts with other scientists, a frame which may be partly altered by what he places inside it. His procedure is essentially abstractive, analytic; his observations, hypotheses, inferences and surmises are subordinate to his main desire to achieve a precise, formal, structured account, grounding predictions. The historian instead makes his observations, hypotheses, inferences, surmises and predictions subordinate to a desire to recapture the nature of the past, and to the discovery of the particular path which a process covered in moving from an earlier to a later item in that past. He tries to make his observations fit inside a singular frame, not necessarily accepted by others, which will enable him to give a rational account of the way in which the beginning of a period was transformed into the end of that period.

The scientist looks for what might rationally implicate what he started with, whereas the historian looks for what is relevant to its presence. The one moves from datum to concept, and then from concept to concept, hoping eventually to get from concept to datum, whereas the other moves from present datum to past pivotal item, and then back again (usually only part of the way to some subsequent but past item), in the effort to see what took place within a period of time.

The historian seeks to recover the past. He attends to the concrete, the common-sensical, the observable, in the attempt to learn about the course of the historic. The scientist, instead, seeks a pattern and tries to make it function as an intelligible whole which the particular occurrences illustrate, localize, or help relate to other intelligible wholes. He tries to treat his supposed elements as units in a pattern, putting aside whatever the pattern does not accommodate or enable one to predict.

The tests of the two disciplines are also different. The historian is absorbed in the task of making a host of inferences converge at the same point. His account must be coherent, it must answer to present data, and what he says about the past must be vindicated by what he can learn in the future about that past. (For the vindicational theory of truth see *Modes of Being*, 3.25, 3.26.) But he never can content himself with a conforming to a coherence, a correspondence or a vindicable theory of truth, or combinations of these. He tries to make a number of distinct inferences converge on the same fact. The scientist's stress is quite different. He does not primarily seek to converge on a fact, but to present an account whose implications keep in accord with the course of the world. The one has a theory of truth which is essentially social, requiring the concurrence of many investigators from many points of view—or the concurrence of the different points of view of a single investigator; the other has a vindicable theory of truth requiring of him—and his fellow-investigators —a readiness to confront his structures with those of the world. The scientist wants an account which the world will presumably substantiate subsequently, whereas the historian wants to account for what has already come to be. The latter takes himself to know what has taken place when a plurality of investigations agree; the former takes himself to know what is true when occurrences conform to predictions. It is true of course that an historian works as an individual and that scientists are cooperative. But when the historian works as an individual he assumes a social role, taking many positions; when the scientist works cooperatively he takes a neutral position, offering a pattern which any one might presumably discover, use and know.

The outcomes of the work of the scientist and the historian are also different. The one offers communicable formulations in a neutral language which is open to check by what will take place; the other offers a sociologically oriented narrative in a nonformal language, to be understood only by one who adopts the same outlook. The one expresses in a formalized guise what the world is like, thereby enabling him to predict the nature of some of the occurrences that can be observed. The other is rooted in the present and the relevant past, and orders what he discerns in the light of plausible, reasonable, stable judgments of what men are, and what results when they act inside a world where the past is preserved in and outside the present.

Neither the scientist nor the historian is forced by the nature of things to engage in his discipline. Both, like other inquirers, are stimulated in good part by the views of their colleagues. A good deal of their work is derivative work, a reaction to the reports of others. But initially and in the end both fasten on something in the present which is treated as interesting, either because it exhibits some conspicuous feature, because one's attention terminates in it, or because there is something wondrous about its nature or functioning, place or relations. If as historians we ask ourselves why it occurred in just the shape it did, we will make some use of science. This will enable us to find a differentiating cause or reason for the occurrence. Historians must know something of the causal processes affecting ordinary things in order to be able to explain occurrences as outcomes of stable modes of behavior, complicated perhaps by the occasional intrusion of alien forces. It may prove to be the case that no complication of ordinary laws and processes in nature or daily life will enable the historian to get a final answer to his questions, but he must make some effort to see if this is so. The distinctive nature of what is now encountered may be the result of a contrivance, of a forgery, of a misreading, but all of these have their reasons too. The question of the authenticity of some document is after all only a question about a specific cause and date, other than what we would normally suppose it to have; the decision that a report is reliable is the outcome of the same kind of inquiry as that by which one determines the source of a reliable report.

Science offers an account of what things are. Ideally, it tells us what things will do as a consequence of the unfolding of some pattern. Ideally, too, it is concerned with whatever takes place in public space and time. Ideally, too, it strives towards a perfect clarity and an inherent pervasive rationality. But since it inevitably abandons the objects and occurrences of daily life to concern itself with what, though intelligible, may never be confronted, one ought also to grasp what happens from nonscientific positions as well. History provides one of these positions.

The historian is mainly concerned with knowing what in the past contributed to the presence of the items on which he now fastens. The past for him is not merely what had been present but what in that past clarifies and explains what came after. Anything, trivial or accidental in terms of science, might be of interest to him, having the role of a unit in a chain where it acts as an antecedent condition for what follows after. The historian knows the import of accidents and other occurrences; he sifts out the important from the unimportant in the light of what came later. This is one of the reasons why it is right to say that an historian can often know more about the past than those who lived at the time.

What is focused on in the present is a function of the historian's background and concerns. To begin with, he focuses on what is odd and conspicuous from the standpoint of his daily or nuclear common sense. Later, as one interested in knowing about every aspect of the present, he becomes aware that anything he faces requires and deserves an explanation. In either case he seeks to recover from the past only what is pertinent to the present he has focused on. He ought to go further. He ought to ask if there is anything that requires him to challenge the suppositions that he or others have been accustomed to make about the past. Only then can he be sure that he has done all he should. His objective is a comprehensive account, capable of withstanding the critical examination of himself and his colleagues today and tomorrow.

The historian often makes use of contrary-to-fact conditionals, remarking on what might have happened if causes, which did not occur, had operated. As Pascal observed, had Cleopatra's nose been shorter, the history of the world would have been different. Or, as Toynbee remarked, had Augustine's mission failed, the western world might now have a different religion. The total array of all possible conditionals relating to a public interplay of socialized man with nature, expresses the meaning of an occurrence in objective history.

What actually occurs is something manifested. This can be stated as one of a set of conditionals. It can then be taken to express not merely the manifested but the manifestable, to tell us about the constant root-nature of historic beings or periods. "Because Cleopatra had a long nose, Anthony loved her" explicates the same fact as "Because Cleopatra had a short nose, Anthony did not love her." The one refers us to what took place, the other to what did not; both explicate Cleopatra and Anthony as beings not exhausted in their manifestations. To know what either person really is we must see each in all possible situations and note how the consequences vary with variations in the conditions.

The historian attends to contrary-to-fact conditionals only occasionally, but both when he does and when he does not he assumes that there are no unrealizable historic possibilities. What is never produced in history is, for him, not a genuine possibility. This view of possibility is undoubtedly question-begging, and he makes no attempt to justify it. He is interested only in using it. He may have made an unwarranted assumption, but whether he does or not, he agrees with most of mankind in his belief that man and nature have not yet entirely exhausted their potentialities, severally or together.

2

The Historian's Objective

THERE ARE MANY REASONS why men engage in the study of history. Five stand out conspicuously.

1] Men look to history to learn about their antecedents. All of us find pleasure in such knowledge. Even when we dramatize we express something which is true of ourselves and which it is good for us to know. When our origins are noble we read into ourselves the glories that had been, dimly aware that what had happened is still somehow preserved within the recesses of our being. We are also tempted to enhance our opinion of ourselves and to impress our neighbors, and therefore tend to exaggerate what had been. The excellencies of our past, we suppose, offer some evidence of what one might expect of us thereafter. This supposition would of course be without warrant if what had been was not rooted in the very same nature that we now have, or if it did not play a role in the present, determining what we thereafter can do.

Even where our origins are dismal, miserable, regrettable, there is satisfaction to be gained from learning that we are not the only men whose ancestors have been unfortunate, foolish, wicked or confused. There is a pleasure in knowing that we are not alone, that we are part of a single totality, that we have in a sense lived a long time. A kind of immortality in reverse is achieved by us when we accept what had been, as an inseparable part of ourselves.

There is also a pleasure to be gained from a contemplation of the glories of the past. Sometimes we enjoy attending to them without actually relating them to ourselves. Sometimes we find pleasure in seeing a job well done. We are pleased to take note of the achievements of mankind even when they are only remotely related to what we are or can do. Somewhat as we enjoy the conquests by others of mountains and the arctic wastes, we find pleasure in noting the achievements of cultures not directly connected with our own.

But pleasure, though in a sense offering a terminus beyond which no one ever seeks to go, and which in fact justifies what had been done to achieve it, never provides a sufficient motive for man's basic efforts. Also, were pleasure our objective we could find it more easily and perhaps in larger measure by turning not to the past but to the more evident present, to the more reliable results of logic, mathematics and science, or to the more attractive outcomes of the arts. And since history does not provide a record solely of the inspiring, we would, to find pleasure in it, have to treat the unsavory parts of the past differently from the way in which we treat the attractive parts. We do not, we cannot take pleasure in all we discern of the past, but only in segments of it, or only so far as the past serves some special purpose.

More important perhaps is the fact that the pleasures which history yields cost something. History is the outcome of an inquiry, crisscrossed with errors and confusions. The inquiry is not easy, the errors and confusions are not enjoyable. To engage in the study of history is to be frustrated, defeated, deceived, criticized; it is to encounter much that pains and dismays. History is not given but won.

The pleasure that history provides is on the whole an incidental product of the recovery of the past. Rarely do men engage in it, or in any other inquiry, primarily for the sake of being pleased. If they did, they would still have to distinguish the pleasure found in the activity of the hunt from that produced by a confrontation of the prey, short run pleasures from long, the pleasures that are good from those that are bad.

2]   Idealists, such as Croce and Collingwood, having denied any being to the historic, understand history to be a re-enactment of what had happened. It is true, of course, that we often do want to re-enact what had happened. Holidays and celebrations, pageants, even monuments, ballads, and folklore, renew for us what once had been. The re-enactments help make us more vividly aware of the full nature of our being; they also tear us away from our routine selves and tasks, and enable us, for a moment, to take on the semblance of great men and great events. History, by bringing before us the memorable past, gives us material for desirable re-enactments today.

We do not, however, wish to re-enact the villainies of the past; we cannot re-enact the parts of history which are produced by uncontrolled masses of men or nature. Also, nothing could be re-enacted unless it had first been enacted, and that first enactment is surely historic, the referent of the historical. Re-enactment offers a good motive for the pursuit of history only so far as the past is splendid and within our control.

3] History is an inquiry as well as an outcome. The story which the historian provides is in good part an incidental residuum of an activity, which is his primary concern. Any account on which men have been in agreement for a period awakens the alert historian's curiosity, leads him to probe, to ask questions, to see whether or not his colleagues and predecessors have not slipped unawares into the acceptance of what should have been examined, criticized and perhaps discarded or modified. Like the scientist, the philosopher and the judge, the historian seeks to know what is true; he is not content to rest with the settled, the accepted, the assumed or the believed. His problems are, of course, distinctive. He seeks to date and to place, to determine authenticity and credibility, to find the thread connecting what had been with what is. But like other inquirers, he wants to know, to find out what is the case; when fully aware of this fact, he pursues his inquiry relentlessly, allowing no antecedent commitments, no authority, no established rules or limits to determine what he is to do or where he is to look. His task is to be honest, systematic, critical, to conform to the same demands of integrity and objectivity that are recognized by the other disciplines.

Truth is a powerful motive, driving the historian on in the face of constant frustration and devastating defeat. But truth has many shapes and many values.

To say that the historian seeks the truth does not yet enable one to distinguish him from other equally serious inquirers. And since the truth is more readily and evidently possessed by those who are content to describe, who attend only to obtrusive data, or who make use of those methods alone which preclude or minimize the possibility of error, it cannot be the case that the main reason why men engage in history is that they seek the truth. The historian never arrives at certainty; he rarely ends with more than a not altogether sifted totality of plausible, hypothetical, guessed-at and imagined formulations of what had been. One will more likely achieve more truth by turning away from the study of history than by engaging in it.

To be sure, some truth will be obtained by engaging in historic inquiry, but this usually will be mixed up with the erroneous and dubious. The historian does not find this fact as regrettable as others do, for he is primarily concerned not with achieving pure and well-tested truth but with providing a comprehensive, illuminating account of what had been. Though he would prefer to offer a history free from doubt and error, he would rather present a partially erroneous or unreliable but all-encompassing account than one which had been so purged of the questionable that it was thin, narrow and superficial. If a choice has to be made, he will try to be comprehensive rather than precise or accurate. Were this not the case he would rarely do more than date and catalogue.

The historian seeks to provide a full account. He would like it to be true. He would like to have his work endorsed by other inquirers, and would like to have his results fit in with the large body of more or less settled data whose acknowledgment marks the established professional. Like every other discipline, history has its assumptions, its settled material, its established patterns; only by adopting these can the historian hope to pursue history together with a number of other dedicated students. But as an inquirer he raises difficulties for himself, sets problems and questions to himself. Even if he has an accurate and complete history of some period, he still is dissatisfied if what it says fails to tie in with other things that are known outside his history. Because he too wants in the end not merely a truth in history but a truth for history, or better, a shared knowledge in which the truths of history are but one part, the historian sometimes raises questions for himself which no one has ever asked of him, nor any content provoked. His spirit is therefore quite unlike that of the pragmatists who say that they never engage in inquiry unless there is something frustrating or indeterminate in their data, or of those philosophers who claim that were it not for the paradoxes presented by their colleagues they would never have any problems. There always are some areas which are unclear and perplexing, warranting a pragmatically motivated inquiry; there are always some oddities in the positions of one's colleagues which make desirable a renewed insistence on the obtrusive facts. But men also turn their critical faculties on what is settled and seems most reasonable. It is so easy for us to deceive ourselves, to allow to go unquestioned what does not now disturb, that the resolute inquirer often attends to the very places which the pragmatist and the man of common sense slide over or ignore. The historian is content with nothing less than a comprehensive account, achieved by a relentless use of a disciplined method, taking nothing to be beyond the reach of a critical examination, now and later.

4]   All men look to history to teach them something having value for themselves today and tomorrow. Historians therefore raise questions in addition
to those prompted by a desire to have an account
which can withstand criticism. They look for items
in the past which will serve as clues and guides for
the future. Often they search for well-intrenched patterns, and the warrant for supposing that these will
be repeated or will ground others that will be exhibited later. Men often turn to history as a source
of useful knowledge, and not merely for the sake of
having knowledge as such.

If the world of history were a world of items
which moved forever in fixed ways under the aegis of
knowable laws, there would be no question but that
one could, on the basis of what one had discovered,
say something reliable about the future. Many philosophers today speak as though such laws would be
similar to those which govern nonhistoric occurrences. Some speculative historians, in contrast, suppose historic laws to be distinctive, but go on to suppose also that those laws will, in the future, be exactly
what they had been in the past. The philosophers
overlook the teleological aspects of history; the
historians overlook the fact that the structure of
history is inseparable from unrepeatable content.
That there are laws governing the course of history is
an assumption for which there seems to be little warrant. But if there were such laws they could be
known by attending to present rather than to past occurrences. To know them we would not have to study
history.

Most men make ready inductions from the past to
the future. They infer that what happened to ancient
tyrants will happen to present dictators; they suppose that outcomes similar to those produced by

struggles for power in the past are to be expected from struggles for power in the present. But we have such a pitifully small knowledge of the past as to make any such transference to a new situation most hazardous—putting aside the fact that since the new inherits something of the old it is inevitably altered in promise and activity, thereby defying repetitions of old ways.

A primary and sound motive for studying history cannot be a desire to know laws which enable one to predict or to control the future. Still, something can be learned of the past and utilized in the future. We know that every observable object undergoes change, that there is a constant coming to be and passing away, that nothing remains dominant forever, that the appetites of men come to expression if not in one way then in another, that power needs to increase in order to maintain itself and tends too to provoke the growth of a counteracting power, that the past is inherited, and that there is nothing perfectly good or perfectly bad. These are broad truths, too broad in fact to tell us much about what is to be. But they could serve as guide lines to be filled out with more concrete data, if only we could learn how to translate, into the future, specific truths learned from the past.

One way of making use of specific past truths is by constructing contrary-to-fact conditionals, referred to a while back. These have one of six forms, depending on whether one takes an agent or situation or both to be altered, and whether the result is then similar to or differs considerably from what had prevailed before.

Let us suppose that:

1. *a* in situation *S* yields *b*: (Israel [*b*] owes its origin to Hitler's

laws [*a*] and a Nazi
Germany [*S*])

We then have the following possible conditionals con-
trary to fact:

1) *a* in situation *T* yields *b*:

(Israel would have
come about some-
what as it had
[*b*] despite Hitler's
laws [*a*] even if
Germany had been
differently organ-
ized [*T*])

2) *a* in situation *T* yields *c*:

(There would not
have been an Israel
[*c*], if Germany had
been differently or-
ganized [*T*] though
Hitler's laws were
in effect [*a*])

3) *d* in situation *S* yields *b*:

(Had there been
different laws re-
garding the Jews
[*d*] in Nazi Ger-
many [*S*], Israel
would nevertheless
have come about
somewhat as it had
[*b*])

4) *d* in situation *S* yields *c*:

(Had there been
different laws re-
garding the Jews
[*d*] in Nazi Ger-
many [*S*], there
would not have
been an Israel [*c*])

5) *d* in situation *T* yields *b*:

(Had there been
different laws re-

garding the Jews [*d*] and no Nazi Germany [*T*], Israel would have come about anyway, somewhat as it had [*b*]).

6) *d* in situation *T* yields *c:* (Had there been different laws regarding the Jews [*d*] and no Nazi Germany [*T*], there would have been no Israel [*c*]).

In no. 1 and no. 4 the agent (*a* or *d*) has a dominant role; in the former a change in circumstance (to *T*) is thought to make little difference; in the latter a change in the nature of the agent (to *d*) is taken to have an effect on the outcome (*c*), despite a constancy in circumstance (*S*). One appeals to cases like these when one wants to emphasize the freedom of the agent, or the power of great men or signal events. But they tend to separate the agent (*a* or *d*) too much from the situation (*T* or *S*). In no. 2 and no. 3 there is a reverse stress on the situation; in the former a change in the situation (to *T*) is treated as making a difference to the effect (to change it to *c*); in the latter the original situation (*S*), despite a change in agent (to *d*), is taken to yield a similar result as that which had come about originally (*b*). Here there is too great a detachment of the situation (*T* or *S*) from the agent (*a* or *d*). In no. 5 the outcome (*b*) is detached from both agent (*d*) and situation (*T*); a change in the original agent (*a*) or situation (*S*) has no effect on what comes about. This is the interpretation accepted by those who assume that historic outcomes are fixed in advance; no alteration in what precedes an outcome is thought to be capable of preventing or altering that outcome. But this is to deny that something effective happens in the course of time. The sixth case parallels the initial supposition 1; it presents us with a new situation (T) and a new agent (d) and a correspondingly new consequent (c) of its own. Only it takes full account of the concreteness, the uniqueness, the fixed positions and historic natures of agents (a and d), situations (S and T) and outcomes (b and c). Only the sixth allows for a full translation into the initial case, and conversely. Differences in their respective agents and situations are reflected in a difference in their respective outcomes; what occurred in 1 is an equivalent manifestation of the power which is articulated in the contrary-to-fact conditional (6). The different agents (a and d) and the different situations (S and T) are of course not reducible to one another; they do produce different outcomes (b and c). But the production does involve the exercise of the same power both times.

Contrary-to-fact conditionals are helpful in enabling one to conceive how natures and circumstances of past times are to be altered so that they are appropriate to the present, thereby making possible a prediction of a proportionate change in the outcome that will thereupon ensue. The method has always been used, but in an imprecise and careless way. All of us reason by analogy. We infer that, since tyrannies have always come to an end and often within a decade or so, this or that current dictator will rule for but a short time. We then tacitly suppose that there is only a difference in degree between present and past beings and circumstances, and therefore consequences. Often though they differ in kind, requiring one to make use of some other method than that of simple analogy.

When and as we conceive of an alteration in the nature of something we usually predict a corresponding alteration in its effects. Knowing that the modern dictator differs from the classical tyrant in the size of his domain, the power he can wield, the relations he has to the rest of the world, the nature of available communications, weapons and transportation, we imaginatively modify the old situation until we have it converted into the new. We then predict that the effects will differ correspondingly. But though we can thus make use of what we have learned of the past, we do not know just how much use we can make of it, or where or when. Since we do not know all the circumstances, all the details, or all the actors either in the past or in the present, and since we can never rule out contingencies and free decisions, our predictions will always be hazardous. We can, as it were, predict that sometimes we can predict, and that is about all. This, though better than nothing, does not warrant the expenditure of all the time, energy and devotion that the historian gives to the study of the past. Some historians in fact have gone so far as to maintain that there is nothing which the future can learn from the past, unless it be that there is nothing to learn. Desire to obtain useful knowledge from the past cannot consequently account for them, and will account for most of the other historians only in part.

5]   The most fundamental reason we can have for studying history is that it enables us to complete ourselves in a way otherwise not possible. We men are incomplete beings, always seeking to complete ourselves. This we can do by making other things part of our being. It is tempting to suppose that we can do this by assimilating, controlling, subjugating all things, thereby adding to our substance. But we never physically come in contact with more than a few items, and then only as bodies which can be added to our own. To reach what is outside the grasp of our bodies, and to make it part of ourselves as more than bodies, we must make use of our minds.

Knowledge is a strategy for completing oneself. It can, particularly through the aid of science, reach everything that exists in space-time; through speculation it can encompass the nature of the cosmos and thus in principle make provision for anything that could be. But to know not only what exists but has existed, and then not in purely general terms but in detail and in a shape with which we can and wish to identify ourselves, we must turn to history. There we will find mankind in a plurality of determinate postures, mankind as an actuality, realized, made explicit, ourselves multiplied and our potentialities realized in a way we cannot realize them today, individually or together.

We want to know from history, firstly, how men differ from one another in nature and act—and how they agree. We turn to it to learn how men have behaved, why they have so behaved, and what they are in root and promise. We learn most from history when the contrasts it makes evident are sharp and striking. Such knowledge seems at first to require a denial of the very supposition which the historian makes in order to trace a path through time—that there is a stable nature to man enabling one to provide a plausible link between his different manifestations. Were that supposition rejected he would no longer be able to compare different periods but would have to disjoin them, leaping from one to another by analogy, refined or crude, for only items which have something in common can be compared, and then only with respect to what they have in common. Red does not contrast with square but with green, another color; a square contrasts with a triangle with respect to shape. A comparison is possible between men at different places and times only because they have something in common which the contrasting factors illustrate in diverse ways. The historian can learn how men differ and how they agree only because he retains a grasp on the root identity of them all.

We also turn to history to learn how we today became what we are. From a study of history we learn the difference which political turns, technology, exploration, and even the writing of history have made to our ways, outlook, interactions and aspirations. By making evident to us how dependent we are on the changing character of the world in which we live, history makes possible a more effective control of it. Such knowledge also presupposes an awareness of man's constant nature, for it is only because there is a common core in all of us that we are able to identify ourselves with others and with what they have made their own.

What biography does for the individual, a history does for many, and ideally for all mankind. A biography is a story of one man, presupposing a root identity in him from beginning to end. It uses a man's constant nature to connect his adventures in multiple settings, revealing how he changes his public guises in the course of his career. Similarly, a history acknowledges a constant unchanging human nature which comes to diverse expressions at different times and in different circumstances. An historian, however, is not primarily concerned with knowing what man's constant nature is; he seeks to link the diverse public forms which that nature takes in order that we may know, not what mankind is in principle, but what it is in manifest fact.

History is also an indispensable means for learning what man can do. As we look at man across space we see him in different situations. These are limited in number and range. We need a larger canvas to see the multiple guises he can assume. And some of the guises he can assume are obviously guises which he has assumed. Nothing less than the whole panorama of history will tell us what man is as fully expressed in time. At every moment he reveals himself in a new way. By taking account of the totality of his manifestations, we can have a knowledge of him more detailed and better structured than we otherwise could get by speculation or introspection.

Despite the fact that we today differ from men in the past in rhythm, outlook and goals, we can say that they behaved somewhat as we would have, were we living in their world, and that they would have behaved somewhat as we now do, were they living today. Indeed, if account be taken only of the fact that we and they are different instances of men, we can rightly say that we today behave exactly as they would have, and that they would have behaved as we do. This is of course not the entire truth about them or us; we are, each one of us, past or present, more than instances of man. Each man is unique, individual, and acts in situations in which he never was before and which never will be again. A science might abstract from that concreteness, a philosopher certainly will, but history, though cutting away a host of details, tries to remain with it in its unduplicable, irreducible finality.

History takes account of common features and

recognizes that there is a single mankind which is being diversely displayed over the course of time. It assumes, without hesitation, that men have various drives and sentiments, such as hunger and sex, ambition and curiosity, love, hate and sympathy, and that the different directions, pace and role these exhibit at different times is to be credited to a difference in circumstance. Though one manifestation does have an effect on others, since it is inherited and sometimes even consciously acknowledged and used, all manifestations are for it equally revelatory and ultimate.

At each moment the nature of things is displayed. But what exists also has an unexpressed power, direction and promise, in part because what has been is inherited by it. Beings in the present express a common nature in distinctive ways when and as they incorporate what has been, and permit this to be partly exhibited in the way they are and act.

As a rule implicitly, but nevertheless necessarily, the historian assumes that the domain of history is defined by the peace and prosperity of man, an ought-to-be which endows all occurrences relevant to that peace and prosperity with historic status. If he ignores or distorts this ought-to-be, he will be unable to allow a possible place within his account for those occurrences which, though related to a possible peace and prosperity, are not significant for the present.

The historian can treat the historic ought-to-be as pertinent to all that has already happened, or as pertinent only to some antecedents. If he does the first he will guide his study by an acknowledgment that both the present and the past are to be viewed in terms of their accord or disaccord with the ideal of peace and prosperity; if he does the second, he will take that ought-to-be to have pertinence only to some limited group of people in some portion of the past. Professional historians take some account of the first of these approaches, but only in order to enable them to deal more effectively with the second.

The recognition that a proper perspective on the past must in principle encompass every item, effective or ineffective, desirable or undesirable, requires the historian to acknowledge that the causally ineffective slows up, in desirable or undesirable ways, the appearance of what subsequently occurs in history. The historian does not have to mention every fact, but unless he does acknowledge historical items outside a causal line, he will not be able to remark, as he does and should, that there are occurrences which hinder the coming to be of some outcome. Conversely, one need not suppose that the causally ineffective slows up the time of history; but unless this is supposed one will face historic occurrences which cannot be accorded a place in history.

What is not in a causal line of an ideal peace and prosperity is an *important* obstacle for it. What is not in the causal line of an outcome is, from the standpoint of the ought-to-be, an historic *significant* obstacle for that outcome. What is not in the causal line of some outcome is a *limited* obstacle for it. The important obstacle helps define the *valuational* time of history, the significant obstacle helps define the *causal* time of history, and the limited obstacle helps define the *periodized* time of history. Since the professional historian is primarily concerned with limited obstacles, he necessarily operates within a perspective in which a limited number of ineffective items are given an historic role.

Were the historian content to deal with history as though it were value-free, he would have no need to attend to anything other than what was causally effective. But he knows that whatever has happened in historic time is a possible topic for his history. As a rule he almost unconsciously accepts his own present as that which ought-to-be, or as that which conforms better than any other to that ideal, and therefore treats whatever is outside the causal line of that present as an undesirable hindrance, slowing up the historic time which began with the causal antecedents of that present. But the historian can also take his present (or some past terminus) to be undesirable, and therefore can see various items as offering desirable obstacles to the coming to be of that present.

An historian who looks at the past from the position of the end of the Civil War, understood as the re-establishment of the Union, might take his period to start at any number of places—the firing at Fort Sumpter, Lincoln's election, the invention of the cotton gin, or the U. S. Constitution's acceptance of the fact of slavery. Whichever he takes, he seeks to move back from the end of the Civil War to that beginning, and then attempts to provide a narrative which progresses in a straight line from that beginning to the acknowledged end. His line is in the forefront of a whole range of occurrences whose only historic role is that of hindering the re-establishment of the Union, the overcoming of the tension between the states, the resolution of the question of slavery, and so on. His history offers a causal account of the Civil War as occurring in a larger context of limited obstacles to the outcome that was in fact reached.

3

The Encountered Past

THE HISTORIAN TAKES FOR GRANTED that here and now there are beings which evidence pasts at different distances from the present. He rejects every theory or hypothesis which could take from him the recognition that some beings are older than others, and that they provide testimony regarding a past which is at once operative in and external to the beings which testify to it.

For some, such an attitude on the part of the historian seems arbitrary, unphilosophical, and dogmatic. God, it is sometimes said, could have created the universe just a second ago, with the very items it now contains, all having the very same features, habits, memories and evidences that they now possess. But this contention is ambiguous; at least four different meanings are contained in it: (1) One might be claiming that God can do anything, short of what would involve a self-contradiction.

(2) One might intend to say that if God created this universe at any time, He filled it with beings which were at various stages in their respective careers. More likely what is meant is (3) that no one can tell by looking at present things that they have genuine pasts; or (4) that we err whenever we infer from the present to the past.

The first of these alternatives supposes there is no contradiction in the idea of a present which was not preceded by a past, and presumably might not be followed by something in the future. But a present is a present for a past and a future, requiring it to be related to them. What exists in that present has relations with what had been and what will be. God could not, without self-contradiction, create a present which had no past.

The second alternative takes a creating God to be a deceiver, one who makes some things look older than others, when in fact they are all not only co-present but of the same age. It is a supposition which, strangely enough, is made by many who think of God as having created the universe along the lines of the stories in *Genesis*. When Adam opened his eyes he saw saplings and fruit-bearing trees, new grass and old, cubs and adults. The world he confronted contained apparent evidences of a time preceding the day the beings were supposed to have been created. Faced with objects which were older in appearance, more mature in function, more intrenched in habit than others, Adam had a right to infer that they had had long careers.

The historian ignores both these alternatives as properly belonging to the field of the philosopher and theologian. If, as I think we have good reason to believe on other grounds, the world was not created, they will be dismissed by the philosopher and theologian too (see, e.g., *Modes of Being,* pp. 191–92, 345). Only the last two alternatives have relevance to the historian's inquiry. But they too will not do; in one way or another they deny that the historian can provide knowledge of the past.

The third interpretation in effect denies that we know there are accumulations, growths, decays, or alterations, for the acknowledgment of any of these is an acknowledgment of the reality of a genuine past. That past cannot be entirely sundered from the present; it gives meaning to that present as an outgrowth, a product, or an achievement. To deny this is to embrace a temporal atomism, which maintains that each moment of time is cut off from all the others. Were such an atomism possible, the next moment could conceivably be a moment in which the atomism that had prevailed before no longer held sway. Having denied the obtrusive presence of genuinely older and habituated beings, and thus of the reality of an order in time, a temporal atomism can do no more than say that what it claims is true now may in fact not be true tomorrow (and might not have been true yesterday). The atomism would thus necessarily make provision for the possible existence of a nonatomic world to succeed its supposed atomic one.

No temporal atomism can be necessarily true, since it allows that what it maintains may fail to hold in the future. Having subjected the present to a rather arbitrary interpretation it is a view which can say nothing about what had been or what will be. But there is surely no point in rejecting the obvious if one does not thereby gain some insight into something else.

It is, of course, possible to argue that this is a temporal atomic world, a world in which nothing in the present has a real past to which it continues to be related. But to deny that there is such a past is to hold that the past to which historians in fact infer is not ultimately real. Could such a denial be better grounded than the arguments employed by historians? One cannot embarrass the historian until one can show that an inference to an atomic world was stronger, more reliable than the historian's inference to the past. But this cannot be done, for such a demonstration requires a reliance on memory, an agent much less reliable than the rationally sustained inferences employed by historians. The historian's inferences evidently are at least as sound as those which justify a belief in a temporal atomic world. What right then has one to say that what the historian alights upon is not ultimately real?

Only the fourth supposition has some force. It does not deny that there is a past and that we can infer to it; it denies only that we can correctly infer to that past. But no matter how splendidly a God or an evil spirit manufactured things and no matter how much he tried to confuse us, it would still be the case that we are confronted with older and younger objects. No God or devil could prevent us from inferring from such objects to a past, for to acknowledge something as older than another is to acknowledge just such a past. We can be mistaken regarding that past's nature; we may wrongly date it; we may misdescribe it; but we cannot be wrong, no matter what devils and God there be and what they do, in inferring that it is a past for the present older object.

The only questions that are left apparently are whether or not the past inferred to was itself once present, and whether or not it now has a being outside that present. It makes no difference whether the first of these questions be answered in the affirmative or negative, for in either way we grant that present beings have a past. If that past had never been present it would be wholly new, in content as well as in its pastness; if it had been present it would be new only in its pastness. There seems to be no good reason for taking the first of these answers, and supposing that the past was not once present. Why maintain that the past is a fresh creation, since this would mean that in passing away a present does not become past? Why deny that the present can be referred to at a later time?

The second question, does the past have a being outside the present?, cannot be answered without looking outside history. It is then seen to have a clear, affirmative answer. This it has because of the action of God (see p. 222). Instead of being one who could have made this world without a real past, God then is that being who guarantees that there is a real external past to which we can infer, and which we can report in a history. If God created the universe a moment ago, the one thing He surely did was to give it an external past. That past, on the hypothesis, never had been present. Since from the next moment on, the past would presumably contain what had once been present, the idea of a creating God can therefore assure us only that some segment of the external past was not once present. If we persist in clinging to the idea of a creating God we must then credit Him not only with the creation of present beings but with the creation of an external past which had never been present, and which nevertheless was continuous with and of a piece with a present which had passed away. Such a creating God could never be freed from the charge of being a deceiver of honest, disciplined inquiring men. But once we give up the idea of a creating God we can say that every item in the past had once been present. And this surely is one good reason for abandoning that hoary idea.

Like everyone else, the historian begins with and in the end returns to the present. That is where he finds his evidence. There is no other place it could be. The oldest object in the world is, if present, just as completely here and now as any other. To speak of it as having any age at all is to imply that it did not come into being in the present and that it has relevant antecedents; it is not to imply that it is locatable anywhere other than in the present. The present for the historian is the terminus of processes which began with observable occurrences, went through normal changes and transformations, and terminated in observable occurrences. The past is inferred to from that present. Let an historian, for example, be faced with a document, dirty, torn and yellow, written in an odd script on unfamiliar paper. What he will see will be in the present as firmly, as completely, as unmistakably as the clean sheet alongside it, on which the historian is taking notes. The document purports to tell us about an earlier time when the document was in another state. It appears to be authentically old; its appearance provides evidence to the effect that it had been in a different state at some other time. The document may contain nothing but lies; it may be a tissue of idle fancies; it might even talk of the historian as at the present moment. Unless made just as it is, at the same or a later time than a clean sheet, it will nevertheless be truly old, as it appears to be. Just how old it is may be difficult to determine, but in principle it can be known, just as one can in principle know that what it says is not reliable, by matching it with other known authentic items. (The supposition that nothing whatsoever is authentic is but another form of the rejected supposition that there are no beings in the present which could warrant some inference to the past.)

The document is not simply a yellow paper. It is a yellowed paper, further along in a career of decay and coloration than the clean sheet alongside it is. The historian uses that document as evidence, grounding an inference to the past. Helped in part by the date, by the handwriting, the texture and composition of the paper, and what he presumably has already learned from other investigators about the laws of nature, man and society, he infers back to the time when the document was a white sheet, or to some past time later or earlier than that.

The object of the historian is to know and report what can be learned about the past through a critical disciplined inquiry. To say with Langlois that "there are no historical facts" and that the "historical character is not in the facts but in the manner of knowing them," is to suppose that the historian creates history. It is to confound the writing of history with what the writing is about. If there were no historic facts an historical account would be indistinguishable from an historical novel. One such account would then be no more true than another, but only more coherent, effective, or entertaining.

The historian moves from the present to the past. Unless his problems are artificial he must be forced to move back because of something in the present. He seeks to understand it not by noting the laws it illustrates, the world it makes possible or the neighbors it has, but by learning how and why it came to be. Because any item in the present can be viewed as not fitting in with others, history can ideally be written from the perspective of any item. Because this or that item does not, for some historian, fit in neatly with others today, he finds it necessary to engage in his inquiry. It is these odd items that he usually selects out of the present to ground inferences into what had been. Ideally he could take any item to warrant an inquiry into its antecedents. He could be like the chemist who studies the rare earths with as much attention and industry as he might some more useful and plentiful element, such as iron. But like every other inquirer, the historian makes only some facts the topic of his inquiry.

On the whole the historian is alert to artifacts, objects made by men, which stand in contrast with others that could reasonably or possibly be produced in the present day. His pulse quickens when he encounters some present object possessing traits unlike those characteristic of the newly made. Starting with the knowledge that documents are usually dated when they were written, that men usually write with fresh ink on fresh paper, using the current forms of speech and the vocabulary of a living language, that moss and dust take time to accumulate, that there is a characteristic dress, art, architecture, set of ideas and ideals in a given period and place, he attempts to determine the relevant antecedents of what he confronts. He looks back to the past in the attempt to account for the preparation, production, and claims of the present item, for the presence of it here and now in its present form. He then tries to find a place for other acknowledged items on the basis of their coherence with what he has already identified and independently checked. If an army is in one place at one time and another place at a later time, the historian knows and says that it must have been in some intermediate place in the intervening time, even though he may have no evidence to support that judgment. Gaps are filled in by him on the basis of what he otherwise knows about movements, armies, places and times. He appeals to modes of operation which any man, by the mere fact of living, already knows, vague and incoherent though that knowledge may be.

Any occurrence has *possible* significance for the historian. This fact is missed by those who view history from the perspective of some limited standpoint, such as politics or ideas or power or economics. Historians should be catholic and open-minded, able in principle to take their start with any present item, and able to acknowledge any past item as having an historic role. But different occurrences have different degrees of relevance to one another, and some do not contribute at all to the production of a given occurrence and can at most serve as obstacles, slowing up the course of historic time. This truth is missed by those who attempt to bring into their accounts every fact, no matter how remote or how distantly related to the outcome under consideration. Only an historian who is sensitive to the difference between the important and the unimportant, the causally insignificant and the causally significant knows what to include and what to exclude from his history.

Much of what an investigation into the past lays bare is not used in the historian's narrative. Just what items these are no one can or should try to tell in advance. The antiquarian knows this; he is ideally concerned with the whole field of artifacts even though he knows that much of it is beyond the interest of present or even imagined historians. His work is primarily raw material for those who follow after, enabling future historians to escape, justifiably and with despatch, from the limitations which hemmed in their predecessors. But much of it must be thrust aside at any given period, and perhaps always.

The historian usually tries to date the material which interests him; he would like to determine the time it first came to be part of objective history. This is sometimes a fairly easy thing to do, particularly in the present day when there are so many well-established ways of accurately determining the date of a record apart from the calendar date it may bear. But occasionally it is difficult to determine when an artifact first appeared. To resolve that question the historian must make use of knowledge which had been acquired in other ways. A master of dating knows something of such topics as paleography, numismatics, chemistry, linguistics, and art. It would be going too far, however, to maintain with Freeman that the historian should know everything. That would be to confuse the historian with God. He needs to know only enough to enable him to assign the material to its proper place in space and time. Sometimes a knowledge of chemistry will be all he need add to his normal common-sensical knowledge. Sometimes he need know only the course of philosophy to decide a given case. It is rarely that he needs to make use of more than a few sciences or bits of scientific knowledge in one investigation, and highly problematic that he ever could make use—even if it were available to him—of all that is now known. And when he makes use of scientifically ascertainable truths he does so only as a preliminary to the writing of a narrative in which items are related in a distinctly nonscientific, historical way.

The facts with which the historian begins prompt him to turn back not only to their past but to the beings and the world with which that past is intertwined. In his attempt to check the reliability and congruence of item with item he functions as a disciplined inquirer. In his description of how the facts are congruent, and in his narration of the whole they constitute, he functions as an imaginative reconstructive creator. He then not only collates, but interprets and interrelates his results and the truths they imply.

The most important and difficult task of the historian is the discovery of the nature of the past process by which an acknowledged item came to be. He would have comparatively little difficulty were he the master of every moment of time, each subdivided into units of concordant data, having unmistakable connections with specific units in other moments. But he knows only a few of the relevant items and their bearing on those that follow. He must therefore content himself with tracing a line between the items about which he knows something, and then constructing a plausible account of the intermediaries he does not know and for which he may never have evidence. The intermediaries which he acknowledges must be those which would be required were the antecedent to give way to the consequent in his day and in others as well. Otherwise his account will lack plausibility and fail to clarify. He will not, of course, entirely avoid repeating prejudices and current but arbitrary beliefs. Historical accounts must be constantly rewritten in part because the historian cannot entirely separate an actual historic process from adventitious accretions to it—a fact which is belatedly discovered when his epoch gives way to another. Herodotus and Thucydides not only wrote about the Greeks but as Greeks; the *Decline* of Gibbon reflects his time as surely as it does the time about which he wrote. But because these historians caught something of the essential nature of man in history, we today, despite the limitations we see in them, can read them with appreciation, understanding, and profit.

The distance between past and present fact is the

concern of the historian. He comes to know that distance only so far as he knows what the past in fact was, the kind of power which it originally contained, and the transformations through which beings went, because of that power, until the acknowledged present. He does not construct the past out of the present, but rather reconstructs it, looking to the present for his evidence, and to the future for an ideal which will enable him to know how the past could be preserved in the present. He knows none of these factors with surety, and can therefore hope for nothing more than a reasonable account. But this is perhaps all that can be vouchsafed in any empirical inquiry.

The foregoing can be restated in terms of the leads provided by the *distinctiveness, exclusiveness* and *ultimacy* of some present occurrence. The *distinctiveness* of a present occurrence, its contrast with others which are together with it, leads to the acknowledgment of an *antecedent* occurrence which was modified in the course of the movement to the present. Any distinctive occurrence points us beyond it to a preceding occurrence, and so on without end. An *exclusive* present occurrence is existent and dynamic, tensed towards the future by virtue of its freedom from the past. This means that there must be a past from which it is free and to which it is related as the dynamic to the static. The exclusiveness of a present occurrence, the fact that it stands out, leads us to refer to a *cause* for it. The *ultimacy* of a present occurrence is embodied in its capacity to face and realize appropriate possibilities. Since the present, from the standpoint of some past item, is a possibility, that item is, relative to that possibility, ultimate too. But a past item has no power to realize the possibility it confronts. What is past is as past only a preceding *precondition* for something genuinely ultimate that is to be found in the ongoing present.

Starting with a distinctive present item, we move back to an antecedent, more normal form of it. Recognizing that the present item was exclusive we treat the antecedent as a cause; acknowledging that present to be an ultimate reality with its own prospect, we treat the cause as a precondition. We thus move from what is the antecedent ground of the distinctiveness of the present to the causal ground of its exclusiveness, to end with the preconditional ground of its ultimacy. And then we move forward in a narrative in the attempt to explain the present occurrence with which we began—or some occurrence which intervenes between the acknowledged present and its ground.

Historical inquiry, through the use of present evidence under the control of a disciplined critical use of hypotheses, seeks the credible and authentic base in terms of which some subsequent item and eventually the present evidence can be understood as an outcome. The historian inquires, as everyone else does, in time; his work is part of an objective history. He moves forward into future time in order to learn about what happened in the past. One can therefore, with the pragmatists, speak of him as formulating hypotheses, making predictions and verifying or falsifying these in the future, though what he predicts is not some future event, but either the achievement of knowledge of something which occurred before the inquiry began, or the existence of an occurrence (which he acknowledged in order to move back to a predecessor) derived from the base of an inferred predecessor.

The historian's inquiry has a structure—or more accurately it has two structures, one methodological, the other logical. Its methodological structure is the pattern exhibited by any inquiry. This embraces tentative hypotheses, guesses, constructions, criticism, evaluation, and testing, and a constant reorganization and modification of achieved results.

The logical structure of historical inquiry is the aspect of it which provides the warrant for arriving at such and such a terminus. But history is not logic, and the route inquiry follows (and a history recounts) is not a purely formal structure. We get to the knowledge of the actual past from the actual present by inferring along a route which cannot be defined in formal terms alone. An inquiry in history begins with a particular premiss regarding the observable present, directs us over a temporal distance, and terminates in a particular conclusion regarding the past. The inquiry of history involves the use of a distinctive "material" logic.

The items with which the historian begins are present items standing out over against others. One could look to some peculiarity in the process by which they came to be in order to account for their singularity. To do this is in effect to read back into the past what was troubling one in the present. The historian instead looks to the other present items to provide him with an idea of a normal course of action; he wants to understand the odd item in terms similar to those which make the rest raise no problems, at least for the time being and in terms of present interests. He seeks, therefore, to infer to a past, which could have produced present, distinctive, exclusive, ultimate items, by acting similarly to the way in which normal present items now act. The fact that his inferences refer to a past should not disturb. The warrant and validity of an inference does not depend on the direction one must go to reach the realities in which those inferences are supposed to terminate. Inferences to the past can have as much warrant and be as impeccable as inferences to anything else. Those inferences can be grounded in most acceptable premises, and may follow along lines rationally justifiable.

Inferences to the past are of at least five kinds: inferences to *stadia, predecessors, antecedent components, unifying grounds,* and *orientation points.* All of them have been dealt with in general up to now, under the heading of inferences to the past; it is now time to distinguish them.

Inferences to Stadia: The objects we confront are more than surfaces. They resist, persist, make themselves manifest in multiple ways over a stretch of time. They are substances or are sustained by substances. This underprivileged man, for example, is a substantial man. His status is inseparable from him as he now is. It is not to be held apart from his color, texture, shape, size, weight, health or other features of him, though to be sure one might fight a war to give him a new status, shared by others having a different color. When logicians treat "This man is underprivileged" as a conjunction of two assertions, "This is underprivileged," and "this is a man," they abstract from the fact that his status is now part of the man, not to be separated off by making a logical distinction. This man suffers the undignified role to which he has been made subject. That role is not essential to him, but it is integral to him; it is a feature of him, without which we would not be able to understand many of his public acts. If we wish to stress the fact that the man is now underprivileged, we should say not "This man is underprivileged" or even "This is an underprivileged man" but "This is an under-privileged-man," the hyphen emphasizing the fact that the status and the being who occupies that status, though distinguishable, are not to be separated if we are to give a correct report of the facts.

Though the man is here and now, just as fully as any other being, we find that we understand him better when we treat him as having undergone adventures in the past. We may have watched him for a while and noticed how he lost his freedom. We may have noticed that other men had been denied rights and might suppose that his loss was like theirs. Or we may have noted that he, in contrast with other men, is further along in a process of enslavement. In the first case we rely on memory, in the second on a simple induction, and in the third on an understanding of what it means for a being to have a career of a certain kind. All three provide a ground for inferring from the man as he now is to what he had been, but it is the third alone which is used in the inferences employed by historians.

The recognition that the man has gone through a process of change makes it possible to speak of him in two ways: "This is a man who has become underprivileged" and "This man was once free." The former adds to the "underprivileged-man" the fact that his present has a past; the latter adds instead a reference to the *stadium* which the man once occupied.

A stadium is a position in the past of a being from which a relevant stretch of changes can be said to have begun. The furthest back we can go in this type of inference is to the status which the man once had —to him as a "free-man." Any further step would take us to a predecessor of the freedom (say some other kind of servitude or some other kind of freedom, or failing these, to different occasions in which the freedom could be exercised). An inference to the free-man thus gives us a position in the past from which we can trace a forward process until we arrive at the point from which we began, the present under-privileged-man. We engage in a similar inference when, given the fact that a man was murdered we infer to the time when the killing occurred. We engage in a similar inference when we ask for the beginning of the cabinet system in the U. S. Government, or for the origin of classical Greece, starting in the one case with the present, and in the other with the end of a period which took place some time before our present.

Inference to Predecessors: The free-man at which we arrive by an inference to a past stadium is one who is no longer substantial and is, so far at least, distinct from the man today. He was once a free-man because of what happened in a time preceding the stadium to which we inferred. "Free-man" can therefore serve as a starting point for a new inference back to a being different from the present man,—a being whose actions can account for that man's occurrence. Such a being is a *predecessor.*

If we think of men as linked together in one history of mankind, we can think of an inference to a predecessor as the outcome of a sequence of inferences to stadia. But it is to be noted that such inferences, particularly when repeated over a long stretch of past time, may take us far from present items. Predecessors can be quite different in nature, role and import from their successors.

Inference to Antecedent Components: A man can be subdivided in a number of ways. If we take him in his public role, we can say of him that he there has a plurality of *aspects,* guises, roles, activities which we, by analysis, can distinguish and hold apart from one another. Such aspects, strictly speaking, are demarcated areas, having no independent status. They contrast with the *parts* of a man or of his situation. Parts have a being that the aspects do not have, with powers and natures distinct from the whole they constitute. The right half of a man is one aspect of him, the left another; the cells in a man make up one set of parts, the molecules another. The slave as butler is one aspect of him, the slave as gardener is another; the slave's body, mind, emotions, will, though not found in isolation, are parts of him, exercising distinctive powers and exhibiting distinctive natures. Being bought and sold, denied education, permitted or encouraged to go to church, are parts of the position of a slave. The slave also has *components*. The slave-in-the-slave-quarters, in-the-field, and in-the-master's house are different components of the slave in his characteristic world. These, like the aspects, are on the same level with the man; like the parts, they can be known through analysis and inference. They are items on which one focuses in order better to articulate and understand what is in fact complex. But they do not have distinct natures or powers exhibitable apart from the complexities in which they are found.

Aspects, parts and components can be made to ground inferences to their stadia or predecessors. A study of the predecessors of the parts or aspects, though, will tell us little or nothing about a man taken as a single unitary being. We attend to him as a unitary being only when we attend to the components of him, each of which expresses the full meaning of him in a particular context. We come to know what he had been by inferring to the stadia or to predecessors of his components.

Inference to Unifying Grounds: Instead of beginning with some single item, and ending with a plurality of components which might perhaps be located at distinct places and times, it is possible to begin with a plurality of present items, and from there converge on some single past stadium or predecessor of a plurality. The distribution of slaves in 1860, or the proportion of slaves and free negroes in 1800, leads us back to the location of the docks for ocean vessels, the location of slave markets, the transportation provided by rivers, and so on. Documents, warehouse records, books will ground a plurality of inferences, all ending with the slave trade of the previous decade. We can think of this slave trade as a plurality of distinct interplaying items, but we can also with equal justice think of it as a single occurrence which radiates out into a plurality of component effects from which we can convergently infer to that one past fact.

Inference to Orientations: All the above inferences can be carried a step further. The outcome of each can be oriented in something other than itself. Each feature can be made to have primary reference to some particular object, institution, event, situation, or men; and groups of men can be referred to some such unity as a nation or a state. Since objects change in constitution, numbers and character over time, the number of orientations possible for stadia, predecessors, components and grounds is evidently enormous.

All five types of inference can be made as precise, as exact, and even can be expressed as formally as the inferences employed in other empirical disciplines. Yet no one of these inferences satisfies entirely. We are always haunted by some unfocused doubt whenever we infer to something in the past. We do not altogether trust the inference—just as we never really trust an inference to the existence of God. Suppose one man were to say to another, "I know that God exists." Asked how he knows, the first might go on to say, "I inferred it." Will he not be met with looks of incredulity and sounds of dismay? Would he be able to persuade if he goes on to maintain or even show that his was a good inference, that it was precisely formulated, that it followed familiar patterns of reasoning, that it could have been written with the symbols employed by modern logicians? Would not his companion, with our full support, reply: "I don't care how good the inference is; it won't do. If you want to show me that you know that God exists you must come up with more than an inference."

We don't trust the best possible inference to God. We don't trust the best possible inference to the existence of other minds. Does the situation change when we turn from such inferences to inferences purporting to convince us that there is an external world, that another is in pain, or even that we ourselves have dreamt something or that we truly remember what had occurred? Do we fare better when we infer to the existence of mathematical entities or physical elements? I think not. Nor am I alone. Sceptics, constructivistic mathematicians, behaviorists and materialists—an odd miscellany I grant and among whom I otherwise can find no place —have never been convinced by any of these inferences. Is this because they will not listen to reason? Or is it not rather that they sense that something is missing, something without which one can have no confidence in the existence of God, an external world, other minds, a remembered or dreamt occurrence, the reality of some mathematical entity, or the presence of an intention?

What more is needed? It must either be other inferences or something outside the realm of inference. It cannot be the former, for it is inference itself, not this or that particular one, or this or that particular inference as bringing us to a particular result, which is here found wanting. We'd like to believe the outcome of these inferences, but instead find ourselves dissatisfied with them. Is it that we feel it is inappropriate to infer to these items? But this would mean that we feel, if only dimly, that some areas are closed to reasoning. We might be willing to say that the existence or nature of God is closed to reasoning, but who is willing to say that inferences to mathematical and physical entities are also suspect, that these too are closed to reasoning? If so, what is left, what would be available to reasoning? If not, what warrant have we for allowing inferences to mathematical and physical entities?

A Kantian might say that we have a right to infer only to the gross, macroscopic, experienceable, provided it is the product of an extrapolation from or a continuation of what we now experience. But he then by that edict would have to rule out inferences to many scientific and mathematical entities, for such entities are not experienceable. He would surely have to rule out inferences to the past. He would also have to rule out inferences to other minds or to God, because these too are not experienceable, in the desired sense, and are perhaps not reachable by him by an extension or continuation of what he now experiences. His would be an heroic sacrifice, and yet it would be of little avail. No one is ultimately satisfied even with the inferences which would remain, and which the Kantian seems willing to accept, e.g., inferences to the possible future or to what is not momentarily visible. That is why we want the conclusions of these inferences to be verified.

Some inferences are unwarranted; to engage in them is to go counter to what logic endorses. But even logically respectable inferences fail to satisfy. Almost everyone unquestionably supposes that no inference will suffice to convince him of the existence of God. When sufficiently clear-headed all should as resolutely deny that an inference could convince them of the existence of anything. (Nothing would be gained in giving up a claim to be able to reach existent beings by inference and holding instead that one could infer to features in what is already known to exist. Since an inference to a feature of an existent is an inference to an existing feature, the inference would be as unsatisfactory as any inference to an existent being. Granted that our fellow men exist, we remain dissatisfied with our inferences even if we infer only to their intentions, minds, and feelings, or even only to their colors, shapes or weights.)

Men are well justified in refusing to be content with any inference, no matter how framed, where directed, how supported. Inferences by themselves can only come to an end, and cannot possibly reach something outside the area where they are produced. We are dissatisfied with them because they do not necessarily yield something which can be encountered. We want to face that at which the inferences terminate. This is apparently what the Kantian was trying to say; if so, he distorted his insight by adding the unexamined supposition that one had a right to go outside an inference only if one went to some part of the world which was experienceable in the same way that gross macroscopic entities are experienceable here and now. This is not the only legitimate place to go in order to encounter something. But whether it is or not, for the Kantian too, that at which our inferences end ought to be met with outside the inferences.

We are not satisfied with our inferences unless we are able to encounter the beings at which our inferences terminate. Only if we can encounter the beings to which we infer can we have a sufficient warrant for believing in the existence of God, immortal souls, external objects, other minds, private intents—and past events.

But the past is what has passed away. Granting that it has a being of its own, it seems to be outside our reach. And if we could get to it we would disturb it, make it other than it had been. It never before was that which was reached from our present. Also, to get to it, we would somehow have to be able to travel backwards in time, taking an ongoing time all the while in order to engage in this activity. How foolish then it is to suppose that when we look up at the sky we see a star existing aeons ago. The star as in the past is no longer existent, at least not in the guise it had then. How could we possibly get back to it, granted even the odd supposition that when we see something at a distance we direct our vision to the departed past and instantaneously arrive at something in that past. Sight does not travel backwards; it does not travel at an infinite speed; nor does it alight on what is nonexistent (except when subject to illusions). The past of which the astronomer speaks is not a past which is seen, but a constructed, conceived, mathematically formulated past having no temporal relation to the present in which we now live and see. What is temporally related to the present in which we live and see are common-sensical and historical objects, not scientific ones.

It is sometimes said that the star which we see may have disappeared ages ago. But then what are we seeing? A star which is no longer? If we are to see it, it must somehow remain in being. But then in what sense has it vanished? Does it vanish as an extended, dynamic reality, and yet continue to remain visible but in the past? If this be supposed, those who suppose it are somewhat bolder than some philosophers of history. Croce and Ortega y Gasset seem to believe that there is no past to be known. Thus Croce: "History is contemporary history . . . an act of thought." And Ortega y Gasset: "History is . . . a science of the present in the most rigorous and actual sense of the word." If we follow their lead, we would, as has already been remarked, replace the historic by the historical, the real past by a narrative of it. It is right to affirm that one can see a real star; it is right too to say that a real star in the past can be known and even encountered. It is a mistake to suppose that we get to the star as in the past by opening our eyes. We infer to it so far as it has passed away; but we can encounter it because it nevertheless also is in what is present.

If the past does not exist at all, every inference to it will be in error. If the past does exist but cannot be reached, all attempts to infer to it will be futile. If the past can be reached by inference but cannot be encountered, our claims about that past will dissatisfy even those who make the inferences. Our dissatisfaction will never vanish if we do not encounter the past to which we infer.

The past is no longer present; nevertheless it is encountered in the present. A past occurrence of course cannot be encountered in the way a present occurrence can be encountered; it does not, in the present, have the same nature and role that it had when it had been present. But unless history is not a possible source of reliable knowledge we must somehow be able to encounter the past. As a matter of fact, each of the five inferences signalized above can be supported by encounters with their termini. The inference to a stadium, since it terminates in some phase of the being that is now before us, is in fact sustained by four distinct kinds of encounter. The other inferences, referring as they do to more remote pasts, require help from encounters distinct from these four.

An inference to a stadium is an inference to a stage in the career of a being. It goes from a present underprivileged man to him as in a different, previous state. That previous state no longer is. It cannot now be encountered in the distinct guise it had when it was present. But it can be encountered in the guise of a *power* now manifesting itself in what the man does and is.

We obviously need not attend to the past to know that the man is now underprivileged. But we must make reference to the past if we are to understand why he is underprivileged in the way he is, why his underprivileged status has this shape rather than that, or why it is manifested by him in this rather than in that way. Puerto Ricans are now underprivileged; negroes are underprivileged in the South today in a way different from that characteristic of others there or elsewhere. Both possess their underprivileged status in the distinctive ways they do because of the careers they have had. The past through which each has gone is exhibited in the guise of distinctive powers which make their lack of privilege now, substantial and singular.

Psychoanalysts have seen this point quite clearly. A man, let us say, always stumbles at a given spot.

There seems to be nothing at the spot which could cause a stumble. We might try therefore to explain the stumble in terms of physiological disequilibria, or by referring to physical disturbances too slight to notice. But a physiological account gives us only the parts of the man and situation; an external causal explanation provides us merely with the pasts of some parts, aspects or components. Neither of these will enable us to explain why the man always stumbles, or even more sharply why it is that he stumbles in a peculiar way when he comes to that spot. We must go beyond a mere description of the stumble as a loss of equilibrium, involving such and such tendons and muscles, or beyond a reference to some external antecedent. The psychoanalyst does this; he tries to account for the stumble by looking for something in the past of the man—perhaps some traumatic experience suffered at that spot—which is effective in him now. Similarly the historian tells us about the past in the role of determinants of present acts. Such determinants have a twofold relation to what is present. They are powers active inside the present, and they are facts outside the present at which inferences can terminate. When and as the historian infers to the latter, he attends to the former, encountering the stadium, through which a being has gone, in the shape of an effective distinctive determination of what is now happening.

A stadium is encountered in the guise of an active power expressed as and through present features, natures and activities; it is also encountered in the form of an act of *self-maintenance* enabling a present being to stand over against others, to insist and to resist. The insistence and resistance do not vary in simple accordance with the degree and kind of pressures and influence exerted on the present being. If we take them to be brute facts, or to be functions of the pressure and influence which others exert on the being, we will, in the end, leave the insistence and resistance unexplained. A being resists and insists with different stresses on different occasions because the past stadium acts as a differentiating factor within the being. Whether conscious or not, whether it remembers its past or not, the being responds to what it now interplays with, in the light of what it once had been.

When the underprivileged man was free, his response to his neighborhood, his family, the state, the laws, and public conveyances was other than it now is. He now acts as he does because of the way he once responded. Any structural alterations he might have undergone will not wholly account for the degree and kind of self-maintenance that he now manifests. For one thing, he is differently aware, differently reactive to the same influences that had been operative before. An inference to him as a free-man gets warranting support from the way he now maintains himself over against all else; his having been free is today expressed as a present active power of maintaining himself as the particular underprivileged man that he is.

The desire or lack of desire on the part of men to continue to struggle and to live, to engage in this or that enterprise, evidently has an explanation similar to that of the insistence and resistance of the underprivileged man to present circumstances. In an apparently unchanged situation, a man, without reflection, and sometimes even without self-consciousness, suddenly sinks into despair. The despair is an aspect of his attitude towards the world, an attitude which carries out into the open a stadium through which he had once gone and which is encounterable in the present in the guise of a despairing self-maintenance.

Present beings express themselves today in certain ways because of what they did yesterday. When and as the historian infers to that yesterday he encounters it as effectively expressing itself today as an act of self-maintenance. He also encounters the past in the form of a *directionality,* a kind of purposiveness in a present being. Present beings move and function in ways which no structure or external condition enables us to explain. Such a contention involves a double rejection of empiricism. It denies that one makes an advance towards the observable by abandoning the idea of causality, and with Hume accepting the observer's habits instead, for habit is no more and no less observable than causality is. It denies too that the experienceable is necessarily observable, or that it is identical with what is sensed through the help of the various sense organs. We experience what we encounter, and we encounter powers, dispositions, habits, tendencies, inclinations, purposes, no one of which is sensed or observed.

The past of a being is now encounterable in the form of a directionality governing the expression of the being's nature, features, and activities. There is an ordered sequence of occurrences in it because the being is now expressing a past stadium. When, in acknowledging what is now occurring, we turn expectantly to what will follow on it, we allow ourselves to be carried by a stadium, effectively expressed as a directed sequence of present actualizations. It is, to be sure, we who expect; we have habits of expectation acquired over the years. This fact confirms, it does not compromise the point being made, and for two reasons. Firstly, our habits of expectation are built up through a past successful interaction with other beings. We matched the ordered actualizations of their inherited power with appropriate actualizations of our own. Our habits of expectation thus testify to our previous encounters with acquired directionalities. Secondly, our specific expectations are themselves directionally determined, reflecting the operative presence of stadia through which we ourselves have gone.

We and other beings move into the future now, actualizing these acts rather than those, as the outcome of an ordered present actualization of stadia. In attending to tendencies either in ourselves or in others we attend to a stadium as it now functions in present beings, directing them in this way rather than in that. When and as we note the bent of the things today, we encounter the stadia to which an historian might infer.

Finally, there is a *self-containedness*, a kind of irreducibility to a present object which cannot be accounted for by looking at things alongside, before, or after it. Nor can the self-containedness be read off from the various features which the object exhibits. It is an all-pervasive, an organic truth about it, expressing the fact that what had been undergone serves to keep the object over against all others. Because he had been denied rights, the underprivileged man now has a self-containedness unlike what he had before or what he will have at another time. He now others all else in a distinctive way today because of the present effective operation of a stadium through which he had once gone. This does not of course preclude him from having a constant nature, even a self or soul.

Every present object is encounterable as unique, self-maintaining, directional, and self-contained. If we confront it as having any one of these virtues, we face it as a substance. A substantial being is one whose past relates its depth to its surface, inward to outward; we reach that past when, while observing the outward, the surface, the public act, we face the object as over against us, owning and ordering its outward forms. The way in which it possesses its features, the way it maintains itself, the directed sequence of manifestations it exhibits, and the kind of self-enclosed unity it has are encountered forms of its past stadium. The stadium is now encountered so far as we move beneath the surface which the being presents to us, to that being as owning, insisting on, ordering, and enclosing what we observe.

The predecessors of present beings were once distinctive substances. When those predecessors were present they too had a depth; they too, like present things, acted out dispositions in an order which reflected what they had gone through. But those predecessors can no longer act in this way. To do so they would have to be present, not past. Nor can those predecessors, as a stadium does, act in what follows. Predecessors, unlike stadia, are resident in beings distinct from those now present and encounterable. Caesar cannot act in the document or monument we have before us in the way the stadium of a denial of rights acts in a present underprivileged man, or as a past experience does in a present stumble. Yet if we are to face Caesar as more than the terminus of an inference, we must encounter him, and if we are to encounter him, he must be in the present.

Either the predecessors of a present being (which may be quite remote from it in nature and time) are beyond the reach of any encounter, or we must somehow be able to encounter them here and now. The possibility of a history which can "verify" the outcome of its inferences demands the rejection of the first of these alternatives.

The predecessors to which I infer are conceptualized by me. The conceptualizations provide barriers through which an encounter can be filtered, thereby qualifying the nature of that encounter. By mediating my encounter with a present object by my idea of the predecessor of that object, the effectiveness of the object is given a new meaning, and I am thereby enabled to encounter that predecessor. I so alter the meaning of the object through the interposition of a conceived predecessor of it that I find myself faced here and now with that predecessor in the shape of a modified stadium. Thus, were I aware of a stadium of a monument I would be aware of the way in which the monument was distinguished from other present beings, possessed its features, maintained itself, and stood over against me. Were I to confront that substantial monument with an idea of Caesar, I would face the monument as expressing its predecessor, Caesar.

But if it be possible to modify the nature of an encounter by filtering it through an interposed meaning, what check can we have on our inferences to predecessors? If we had inferred to or merely imagined some nonexisting man and used this as an intermediary when we were confronting this monument, we would have just as effectively qualified the nature of the encounter with the substantial monument as we did when we used the idea of Caesar as an intermediary. Any idea, it would seem, could provide a qualification of the encounter which a stadium in a present object provides.

It surely is true that any idea whatever could be used to qualify the nature of an encounter. But an intermediating idea of what was not a predecessor will not lead us to qualify an encountered stadium in such a way as to give us an encounter with a predecessor. If we did not know how to select ideas which were in fact conceptualizations of actual predecessors, and thus were appropriate to what we confront, we would unknowingly distort our encounters, and perhaps refer to what had never been. The intermediating ideas we must use must therefore be known to be ideas of predecessors. We must first legitimately infer to Caesar before we use an idea of him to qualify the nature of what we now encounter. Such legitimate inference is of course possible. (The trouble we found with inferences before was not that they were in error but that they required supplementation, that they demanded completion by means of an encounter.) And we can know that an inference to a predecessor is legitimate if it concludes with a predecessor from which one can move in a direct causal line to the present from which we inferred. When and as the historian infers to a predecessor he uses the idea of it to qualify his present encounter; if he has correctly inferred to a predecessor he succeeds in encountering that predecessor in the guise of a properly conceived modification of an encountered stadium.

Strictly speaking, then, what we do when we encounter a predecessor is not radically different in principle from what we do when we encounter a stadium. To be sure, the stadium is an earlier stage of the being now confronted, whereas the predecessor might be radically different from the present being, and none of its states or features may be like those possessed by the present being at any time of its career. Still, we know the stadium through an inference, and we mediate our present confrontation with a being by the terminus of that inference. Both the inference to a stadium and an inference to a predecessor are thus supported by an encounter filtered through concepts arrived at through inference.

An inference to antecedent components is faced with the same problems as one which moves to predecessors. But in addition it is up against the fact that the components to which it concludes are themselves often diverse in nature, and cannot provide a qualification to be imposed on what we now encounter. Ruins are the outcome of the juncture of bomb and cathedral. The antecedents of the ruins are the cathedral constructed in such and such a way out of such and such material, and the bomb as having such and such a charge and exploding in such and such a place. The antecedents are not the bomb or the building in their concreteness, but components of these which are ingredient in the actual cathedral, in the bomb as it is hurled through space, and in the two together. Those components do not of course have the nature nor the power of the bomb, the cathedral, or their combination. Our present encounter is an encounter with the components of the ruins, when the encounter with the ruins is qualified by our ideas of those components.

Not only can we encounter a plurality of antecedent components, we can encounter antecedent unifying grounds for a plurality of present encountered beings. Observed ruins are scattered over a hill; available documents narrating one and the same incident are found in many archives. The ruins and the documents are the effects of unitary occurrences, dispersed in such a way as to preclude the presence of those occurrences in any one of the effects. We appear to have no way of adding to an encounter with one of the effects of a unitary antecedent, an encounter with other effects of that antecedent. The present items do not seem therefore to permit of an encounter with what had been their common ground. Those items, however, are not mere elements in an aggregate; they are in a single spatial field. We can infer to their common antecedent if we do not deal with them severally or as bunched together by us, but as located in a spatial field. And we can encounter that common antecedent as that which makes the present into a unitary locus of the dispersed items. The unitary ground for a plurality of present items is thus encounterable in the spatial field in which the evidence for that ground is to be found. The field is what that unifying ground has become in the present; in attending to that field as distinctive, possessive, tendential and self-contained, we encounter the unifying ground.

The unitary Caesar I construct on the basis of the available dispersed evidence, if it is not to be the construction of a faint image of a man, must envisage him as having heart and lungs, blood and tendons, and as passing through various intermediary points between signal places. To make Caesar most human I therefore must go beyond the facts to what, so far as the available evidence is concerned, might be only a fiction. This need not disturb, however, and for two reasons. As was observed before, we make our constructions plausible by imposing them on present encounters and then taking account of the way the encounters are modified by being filtered through our ideas. Secondly, the additions we introduce, and which go beyond the evidence, make it possible for the evidence and the inferences from the present encountered things to be integrated in an intelligible, reasonable way.

It is rarely that we are content to remain with inferences to a stadium, predecessor, component or ground, even when backed by encounters. The results have too cold a sense, are too detached in meaning to interest us for long. We therefore seek to qualify the outcomes of these inferences with references to central, focal or important objects. These objects are in the past. But that means they are effete, powerless, alien. To make them vital, intimate, of arresting value, we must make some present being function as an orienting point for them. That being will cast over them some of the radiance it enjoys as a present reality. And there is no better orienting point than an historian.

Sooner or later what the historian encounters is referred by him to himself as undergoing and qualifying those encounters. That historian represents the rest of us so far as he knows, judges and acts in ways that illustrate rules, conditions and criteria acceptable to us all. He can, so far, orient the past for all of us. The recognition that he represents us enables him to know what his encounters mean for all. The historian escapes solipsism and idiosyncratic reconstructions, thus, not only by attending to the evidence and trying to do justice to it, but by offering representative orientations for his encounters. It is the outcome of his representative, not of his idiosyncratic encounters which he reports.

There is much in this analysis which is close to what Whitehead apparently had in mind when he spoke of the objective immortality that things achieve when they perish in time. His account, however, is closely tied to his thesis (inherited from Descartes) that actual occasions perish as soon as they have come to be. That thesis at times prevented Whitehead from affirming that there were any beings, other than God, which actually persisted. As a consequence he was not able to explain how anything could be self-identical over the course of an individual life, how any man could be guilty for something done by *him* years ago, how there could be obligations, political action, physical motion, artistic production or an historic process. But what he said about objective immortality can be detached, I think, from his odd though regrettably central thesis that actual occasions perish as soon as they have come to be.

The past is at once outside the present and in it. As outside, it can be reached by inference; as inside, it can be reached in an encounter. When the historian both infers and encounters that to which he infers, one of his inquiries is over. But he still has to write down his results, and describe a course of history from the inferred past to the encountered evidencing present, or to some point in between. It is an essential part of his task to provide an historical narrative.

4

The Historical Narrative

WERE THE HISTORIAN CONTENT merely to discover truths about the past and then to communicate the result, he would be engaged in a reputable enterprise. But he does more. He presents important truths in a creative composition. This achievement distinguishes him from the archivist.

Evidence which may not loom very large in the present may point to a past event having great value in helping us understand what men have gone through. The records of long departed civilizations take up little room today, and are rarely studied except by dedicated scholars, but they provide a ground for an important retracing of the development of mankind. In contrast, the explosion of the population into the countryside on a holiday is a striking event, but it does not normally arrest the attention of the historian, since it can be readily accounted for by attending to the opportunities offered by roads, cars, the closing of businesses and the like. To be sure, the holiday does provide evidence regarding great events in the past, and the celebrations of today bear within them something of the celebrations of previous years, but the historian has more illuminating items in the library which he could use were he interested in understanding either the initial occurrence or the history of celebrations of it. Normally the historian is attracted by a striking event that affected a great number of people for a considerable time. Sometimes it is only the numbers which excite him, and sometimes it is the stretch of time over which an event has continued to affect men, but as a rule he is attracted only to conspicuous occurrences having both features. Mass migrations may awaken his interests, and so may the invention of the horse collar or the cotton gin, but these are really side or partial issues. The horse collar is to be noted if it helps him build up an account of the conquest of Rome, the growth of manors, farmers and an urban population, the cotton gin if it helps him trace basic changes in the economy of the South and its altered relation to negro help, and the like. And when the historian writes his account of these and similar massive occurrences, he attends to their most signal turns and patterns. A representative of all of us, he seeks to possess, and thereby to give to mankind, the past through which it has gone.

The historian offers no mirror of what has happened. He tells us about the historic world, but as subjected to and qualified by conditions imposed by inquiry and communication. Sooner or later he turns his back on the historic world and sits down in his study to write a narrative. This is guided by the idea of *relevance*, the desire to *periodize*, and the need to *dramatize*.

An occurrence is relevant to whatever requires it as a precondition, provided that the conditioned, is itself a precondition of that for which the occurrence is not a precondition. Rain is a relevant antecedent for mud, so far as the rain is not relevant to the delay in an army's advance for which the mud was responsible. The delay in turn offers a reason why supplies were not replenished, and makes the mud irrelevant to the failure of the supplies; this in turn tells us why the battle was lost and why therefore the failure of the supplies is not relevant to what ensues on the loss of the battle. What is relevant to the loss of the battle is not the rain, not the mud, not the delay, but the failure of the supplies. Had there been no rain the supplies might still have proved to be inadequate, and even though there was rain, the supplies might have been made available. The import of the rain is absorbed in the mud, so that the rain is no longer relevant to the delay that the mud made possible. The mud transforms the rain so that it is no longer an isolatable factor capable of conditioning the later occurrences.

Occurrences have significant beginnings and endings. It is not necessary for the historian to start with the coming of man and to end with the present day, nor is it desirable. It is possible of course for a relevant item to remain comparatively unaltered through time. It can remain in the result it makes possible with somewhat the same character and power that it had before that result ensued. The faith in the efficacy of reason runs like a thread through the sermons, social theories and philosophy of eighteenth-century England, almost unaltered despite miltiple setbacks and counterattacks. But so far as it brought about one effect it was not relevant to what came later; a reassertion of the very same conditions was needed to make those conditions relevant once more.

The idea of relevance helps the historian to periodize his history. He makes use of one or more of five units—the *event*, the *episode*, the *chain*, the *period* and the *epoch*. An *event* is the smallest historical unit. It is a single occurrence, the division of which into earlier and later items would destroy the unitary meaning and being of the occurrence. There are events which take ages to complete—for example, the career of mankind. And there are events which are so brief that nothing could be smaller, and thus which constitute the ultimate elements of natural time. From the standpoint of history the former would make much too long a unit and the latter one much too short.

Different histories take different types of event as their units. One of them may speak in terms of battles, another in terms of wars; both of them will deal with real beings which function as beginnings, as endings, as conditions, or as powers which ground and come to expression in the events. Since every event is entirely in the present, and since a war nevertheless encompasses a number of battles which occur one after the other, we are faced with the problem of reconciling the different and apparently incompatible types of events studied in different histories. The reconciliation, however, is not the topic of history proper; it belongs either to a history of history, or to a philosophic study of the historic world. The former offers but a stopgap, for the event in a history of history, in which the war and battles are a part, must be reconciled with the war and the battles, as well as with the events demarcated in a history of history of history, etc. The philosophic study, in contrast, presupposes an understanding of the nature of the historic present, and must be deferred to the second part of this book and its discussion of the nature of historic time.

An *episode* is a sequence of at least two events in which the beginning of one is irrelevant to the ending of the other. Rain, mud, and delay constitute one episode, delay and the failure of supplies another. The delay, as determining the failure of supplies, forces the mud and rain into irrelevance with respect to those supplies. The failure of the supplies begins an event which ends with a change in internal policy; the failure of supplies thereby makes the delay (which was relevant to that failure) irrelevant to the change in policy.

History has a rhythm because there are episodes. The episodes may follow one another without interval. They may be of short duration or long. The beginning of each defines the episode's antecedent to be irrelevant to the episode's successor. Were there no episodes, as some men on behalf of the idea of continuity maintain, written histories would in good part be distortive, and the historic world would be one flat continuum of occurrences. But there do seem to be sharp turns in the historic world, real episodes. The acknowledgment of these need not be accompanied by a belief that history breaks off at various points only to start up again almost at once, or that there are only cataclysmic endings, requiring whatever follows on an event to have a new weight and meaning. Episodes follow hard on one another, and what ends one may not be much different from what ends another.

An historic *chain* embraces a sequence of episodes. Each of these episodes, with its characteristic beginning and ending, belongs to the chain so far as there is some character which it shares with the other episodes. There are many historic chains, beginning and ending at different times. All that fall within the same stretch of time constitute an historic *period*. An historic period need not contain a single chain as long as itself, and parts of a number of chains within one period (or the chains themselves) may all occur at the same time. The historic period of the United States in the major portion of the nineteenth century is one in which there are distinct historical chains whose concurrent episodes embrace the shrinking of the frontier, the growth of suffrage, industrialism, the extension of political freedom, and the expanding power of the courts.

An historical report tells about an episode or two; an historical monograph relates to a chain; a history deals with a period. The beginning of the period is relevant to the end, and provides a common factor for the different chains which the period contains. The growth of public education may be the common factor of a single period characterized by an increase in the number of published books and newspapers, new legislation and religions, the shift of population and so on, each of which is part of a distinctive chain in that period. The chains may affect one another; but whether they do or not they are part of a single history because conditioned by the same antecedent periodizing factor.

Histories of art, science, philosophy, of inventions and discoveries can be thought of as facets of a wider history which embraced all the major activities of men. But as a rule, these histories are dealt with in abstraction from political, economic, social and military occurrences. They are then distinct chains separated from their own predecessors or successors by empty or chaotic episodes. One chain will usually encompass the work of only one individual or a school, to be dealt with in the light of some outstanding achievement, a professed objective, or a particularized form of an ideal for that discipline.

Since there is often more than one outstanding work in a given field and since objectives are rarely professed, the historian of ideas is usually forced to deal with a number of chains, and to treat all of them as being governed by some such ideal as a standard of beauty, verifiable or speculative truth, or the presence of a creative mind, spirit or body. To make provision for the fact that most great work appears in a context of lesser works, and often develops along a path set in more or less deliberate opposition to those prevailing, a history of ideas should also take account of the interplay of the new with the established, and make an incidental or derivative reference to a dominant figure or movement. The study of Plato's philosophy, Rodin's sculpture, Flemish painters, modern physics, inventions and explorations, if held apart from the contrasting prevalent activities and achievements, will tend to degenerate into biography or chronicle. They should be interrelated with other events, patterns, and tendencies.

An historic *stratum* is a set of concordant and contemporaneous occurrences. A period of history encompasses a sequence of historical strata in which concordant events are quickened by common conditions. Napoleon with his ambition, contemplating the weakness of neighboring countries, and backed by the enthusiasm of his soldiers and the armaments at their disposal, is part of one historical stratum; Napoleon at Waterloo occupies another. The two strata are part of one history, not because Napoleon is in both but because they are conditioned by some such common factor as the weakening grip of classicism, the backwash of the revolutionary spirit, the growth of imperialism, and the like.

An historical stratum is a portion of the world frozen at a point in the past, and serving as a base for inferences backwards or forwards. It offers a cross section of a number of episodes, cutting different episodes at different points. No stratum reveals what preceded it or what will follow after, for each contains portions of episodes and thus is only an analytic element, without genuine being, without a genuine past or future of its own. At the moment that Napoleon's ambition was at its climax, the enthusiasm of his soldiers was apparently increasing, while his neighbors were making amends for their previous weaknesses. All three episodes belong together in one historic chain of strata. The outcomes of one or more of these episodes may be caught within a stratum in which the outcomes of other episodes are to be found. The different outcomes, though they may have distinct origins and have come to be in that stratum by independent routes, may thereafter interact with and affect one another. No historian can safely look simply forward or backward and ignore all that is to the side. Conditions which governed a few episodes at one moment govern a multitude at another. Historical chains and periods swell and contract in the course of time.

Because we usually signalize a stratum by a date, we tend to treat the stratum as though it were more real than the episodes it cuts across. We can avoid this error if we treat the stratum not as a straight line but as a plane which varies in breadth and contour so as to enable it to include only complete episodes. An historian of the beginning of the nineteenth century will therefore go back fifty years for his initial starting point in his account of ideas or art, and only a year or so for his initial starting point in his account of inventions or discoveries in trade or land, even though the latter may have a long objective history behind them.

The largest unit of history is the *epoch*. This encompasses a number of periods whose units are episodes. The epoch is to be understood as spending itself in the realization of some possibility for an entire people. It will be succeeded by another epoch having its own prospect. Only a rare historian is interested in more than one epoch, though the history of mankind cannot be encompassed in only one. The historian must therefore either see the epoch he studies as offering a paradigm in terms of which he can measure all others, or he must take himself to have written only a part of a history and to depend for the rest on the work of others. Every historian leans sometimes towards one of these approaches and sometimes towards the other. He cannot avoid taking the epoch which he knows best to serve as a model for understanding other epochs. But he must avoid provincialism and he must avoid ghettoizing. He can escape the first by allowing that all epochs are presumptively worthy of an historian's attention, and he can prevent the second by understanding his own epoch to be exhibiting the same human nature that other epochs do. Since he knows there is a future now being made present—indeed that he himself in the writing of his history may be about to make a contribution to that incipient present—he must also see his epoch to have an historic role, which some subsequent historian may come to know.

Though both the historic and the historical have their turning points, ending limited chains of relevance and beginning new ones, only the former is without gaps. Event follows hard upon event and all the events together, when they pass away, make up one dense past. But the historian never knows more than some items in the past, and even when he knows a number which flow one into the other, the nature of his discourse, the very breaking up of his knowledge into words, sentences, paragraphs, chapters and books, forces him to hold apart, detach what was not in fact separate. To overcome this defect he dramatizes. He acknowledges powers, drives, directions, takes account of substances having promise and careers—refusing, in short, to be a mere phenomenalist, i.e. one who tries to begin and remain solely with what appears.

Phenomenalism can be of many types. It is possible to take phenomena to be externally linked, disconnected without effect one on the other. They would then not only have nothing to do with what might lie alongside but also with what might lie behind or before them. This would not preclude the historian from bringing various items together in bundles to make newly constructed unities of some interest. But what he then did would not answer to the supposed facts. Or phenomena might be held to have some relation to one another, but not to make an intelligible pattern. They could be in a jumble, appear at haphazard as it were. Or phenomena might be thought to be connected by correlational or functional laws. If we adopt this hypothesis phenomena would be supposed to exhibit such and such a relation or pattern; they would not be taken to exert pressure on one another. But since the relation and pattern would not be grounded in the phenomena, neither could reveal anything beyond itself—and could wrongly lead us to suppose that it does. Most important, such a phenomenalism leaves no room either for a genuine coming to be, or for any objective, rational order. According to it, things just happen to occur in contingent patterns, or in correlatable ways. None of us in fact ever sees such phenomena. We all live in a world in which beings persist, act, react, suffer, have careers and pass away, in good part in predictable ways. And the phenomena we note are all inseparable from more substantial, encounterable realities.

Still, it is the case that the past is made up of dessicated facts. The past is completely determinate, completely manifested, without potentialities, without any capacity to change or to become. It is what a present has left behind, no more, no less, no other. He who attends only to its several items refers to nothing other than what is phenomenal. The phenomenalistic approach has therefore some justification when confined to what is wholly past. Nothing acts in the past, nothing insists on itself there. Each fact is without power to affect or to be affected. It once was, to be sure, part of a vital causal movement, and even now is under the governance of a final cause rooted in the present. Since a phenomenalist ignores such causes he must be content to provide a chronicle rather than a history.

A chronicle re-presents sequences of phenomena, as they are in the past. To do justice to the fact that men are causal agents, and that their motives, purposes, intents and habits have a role to play in what occurs, one must do more than chronicle; one must produce a narrative. The narrative offers hypotheses designed to enable one to understand, on the basis of what had been, why such and such occurs. It re-orders data, stressing some and minimizing others in the effort to explain and clarify. He who does not provide such a narrative has not yet completed a history; but to provide one he must acknowledge meanings, powers and tasks beyond the interest or capacity of phenomenalists.

The artistry of the historian is shown in his ability to lead his readers beyond the recordings of a chronicle as well as beyond the divisions of his own discourse, so as to make them aware that the past, though it contains no genuine breaks, does contain vital distinctions, turning points, and periods. His artistry is something like that of a novelist or a playwright, who tries to drive his audience past the divisions of his discourse, and to accept a book or play as an articulated or manipulatable unity. And like the novelist and playwright the historian is inclined to attend to pivotal figures, to employ unexpressed norms, to give different weights to different items.

The least the historian should provide is a history of mankind for a period or an epoch. He sometimes speaks of such a history as a history of civilization. But it can offer us only a fragment of the history of civilization, a partial account which mankind might eventually complete. Let us, though, for the time being accept his terminology. If we do, we can say that a civilization has three essential constituents—outstanding effective men, a unifying tradition of worship or belief in some desirable final state or value, and a standard of right and wrong—all governing the activities of a people. Any one of these constituents may be dominant in a given civilization. All of them may be mixed in many ways; each may undergo considerable change in the course of time.

A civilization may be usefully characterized in terms of the dominance in it of leaders, outlook or standards. Those whose natures are determined mostly by leaders are secular civilizations; those whose natures are mainly determined by a unifying tradition of worship or belief are religious civilizations; and those whose natures are largely determined by standards are moral civilizations. Sometimes one of these factors comes to the fore with such power as to make the others into subordinate expressions of it. When Christianity was dominant, the greatness of man was exhibited by the saint and not by the hero, and right and wrong was defined by the church and not open to the judgment of ordinary men; but in classical Rome where the hero was dominant, religion was seen to be pivoted in him, and right and wrong were either defined or arbitrarily determined by him.

A secular civilization contains outstanding men who qualify the fact that groups publicly interplay with one another, with institutions, with the energies contained in those institutions, and with nature. Only a few individuals in any secular civilization have any magnitude, or make any significant contribution to the continuation, the increase, the decline or overthrow of the civilization. And the great men, though they stand out over against the others, are also to be numbered among the rest, for though they help characterize a civilization and do lead their fellowmen, they are also conditioned by their civilization and the men they lead.

Should there come a time when there are no outstanding men, no unifying religions and no standards, a civilization either will break up into sub-civilizations such as the army, business, market, or it will be followed by a time of chaos and confusion. In either case we will have an interregnum in the history of civilizations. That interregnum may have a long duration; the people in it may have a constant nature; some great works of art or thought may be produced in it; but it will be insufficiently unified to be a civilization.

In a secular civilization certain men dictate what all the others—the people—do, and subjugate religion and ethics to themselves. The Golden Age of Greece, the time of the Roman emperors, the Napoleonic era, the world carved out by the American founding fathers were secular civilizations. Today Khrushchev defines one secular civilization and de Gaulle another. By an extension one can speak of secular sub-civilizations, dominated by men engaged in some limited enterprise. Bach, Shakespeare, Yeats, the Robber Barons all define sub-civilizations of a secular type. By an extension in another direction one can take a civilization to be dominated by a succession of men, all of whom are imbued with the same or affiliated ideals. There is a Russian civilization defined by a succession of Czars, and another by a succession of leaders beginning with Lenin and still continuing.

A people led by leaders is a guided people, even when it is unaware of these leaders or is unappreciative of them and sometimes even openly defies them. The leadership is not necessarily exercised directly. It may be mediated by laws, institutions, functionaries, or by a control of economics, transportation, communication, rights and opportunities, and even by other men. In ethical and religious civilizations a people is as firmly guided as in the secular, but usually needs to be supported by men habituated to conform to institutions, rituals, and prescribed sacramental patterns. In those civilizations, the leaders do not act primarily as men who control or master others, but as loci of values or as bearers of standards.

A people exhausts its actual nature and meaning in the time in which it is. To suppose otherwise is to treat it as a number of men, not as a people; it is to see it as outside the given civilization and thus as distinct from the actual, historic reality that it was for a time. When a civilization passes away, so does its people; when a people passes away so does its civilization. The character which a people has over against others is integral to the civilization of which it is the body. As historic, a people is no more or less or other than what it is and does; it could not in fact be more or less or other than it is without ceasing to be the people of that civilization. This does not mean that a people fulfills itself, does all it ought to do. Firstly, since one people gives way to another, it must have potentialities which are realized in the shape of the people that replaces it. Secondly, what it does and the way it gives way to another may be much less than could have been. The powers to be found in a people are not exhausted in any limited time or civilization. But a people's nature is fully expressed and exhausted in its civilization, where the latter is understood to include the transformation by which the civilization produces its successor.

The public, ordered, periodized juncture of different segments of a people with one another makes up the history of that people. A civilization can therefore be said to have a history of its own, if it is treated as the product of conflicts, wars, antagonisms and interplays of different segments of the people with one another under the governance of leaders, a religion or ideals. When we turn from the civilization to the transformation of it into a succeeding civilization or an interregnum, a people and its civilization function as unities grounding either another people and civilization, or as a plurality of items whose interplay may produce such unities.

The relating of one civilization to another, the comparing of them as better and worse, the reference to ideal men, to a religion or to an absolute ethics for principles in terms of which civilizations can be scaled is, properly speaking, outside the province of the historian of a civilization. An historian need not, to be sure, confine himself to only one civilization; he need not be oblivious of the need to compare and evaluate civilizations, or of the existence of standards which lie outside the sphere of a corroding time; but if he does take account of these he will have become either an historian of mankind or a philosopher of history. He is not yet ready to become the one, though this is an ideal he ought to realize. He need not become the other. But still he ought to know something of what the historic world is like, apart from what a history can say of it. The historian should study the philosophy of history to learn about the reality and dimensions of the historic world, if only in order to see whether or not he can get support for what he thinks might have occurred in the past.

II

THE
REALITY AND DIMENSIONS
OF THE HISTORIC WORLD

5

Nature, Man, and the Historic

A PHILOSOPHER who is interested in lived, i.e., objective history, does not attempt to discover what in fact happened, nor to recount what he thinks was the course of the world. He seeks to deal with history in one of two primary, not necessarily altogether compatible ways—as that which does, must or ought to exemplify some fundamental power or category, or as the product of an interaction of nonhistoric items. The one approach yields a philosophical history, the other, a speculative philosophy of history. The topics of the philosophy of history are more basic than those that concern a philosophical history; it need not support or justify any of the claims made by philosophical historians. It might even deny that a philosophical history is possible on the grounds that there is no power which objective history can or does express or illustrate.

Hegel, Marx, Schopenhauer and Jung are philosophical historians. For Hegel, history is a function of a single world spirit; for Marx, of dialectical matter; for Schopenhauer, of a will; and for Jung, of a single collective unconscious. Each sees the occurrences of history, severally and together, as loci or products of cosmic powers, somewhat qualified, fragmented and disordered. Most working historians are more conservative. They attend to much smaller areas —usually nations and states, and for a period or so. Following Vico they suppose that different nations and states express different "tempers" or "spirits." In principle their view is like those of the preceding thinkers, differing from them only in that they suppose there are many distinct "spirits," thereby preventing an explanation of the whole of history in terms of any one of these alone. Collingwood, the only distinguished philosopher in recent times who was also an historian, sided with the working historians and held that a plurality of powers was exhibited in history. Each individual, according to him, has its own inside which it exhibits in a single occurrence or in a limited set of them. His view has serious defects, but it is, I think, sounder than that held by most philosophical historians.

There is no warrant for the tacit supposition of most philosophical historians that the three ranges of power—cosmic, national and individual—are incompatible. It is possible for all three to be exhibited at the same time. The power might for example be cosmic in itself and divide first into subordinate national powers and then into individual powers. Different nations and different individuals would then, while acting in independence, be united in root, offering variants on a single theme. Together they would articulate a cosmic power which a philosophical history might suppose was the source of all that occurred.

That power could be purposive, blind, or dialectical; it might be expressed with clarity or obscurely; it might control or spend itself in the act of exhibition. It could allow for a continuum of occurrences, for periods in history, and even for atomic events; it could be expressed haphazardly or allow chance to have a role. It could, as Kant suggested in his *Critique* in another connection, exhibit itself with freedom at the same time that occurrences were being produced in a necessary sequence. It could justify predictions; it could be good or malicious; it could be thought to have any one of a multitude of possible shapes, insistencies, rationales. It might be known antecedently to the occurrences it was making possible (which is what philosophical historians sympathetic to metaphysics seem to believe); or it might be known subsequently (as some empirically tempered philosophical historians seem to hold). But whatever the nature of the power be taken to be, whatever the mode in which that power is said to be known, the philosophical historian is apt to slide too readily over the fact that historic events have their own rationale.

Philosophical history does insufficient justice to the truth that what happens today is relevant to what happened yesterday, and is not merely its successor, or another illustration of a common power or principle. It is not even enough to say, as most philosophical historians do, that history is an effect of the action of a power which is directed towards some end, for this still allows that the future might not have any bearing now on what had been. Philosophical historians also fail to do justice to the fact that men respond to the results of history, and that they alter their courses in the light of what they have learned of the past.

Whatever exists shares with others at least the fact

that it is, that it is conditioned by and conditions others, that it has some relation to still others, and that it probably bodes well or ill for man. But it is a large and hazardous step to move from this to the view that the historic is the expression of some relentless power or powers. The historic world is the outcome of fresh junctures of groups of men with external forces; it is not the result of some imposed compulsion. Beings in history, to be sure, also have reality outside history. But it is only so far as they are in history that they can determine what shape the historic world is to have. And then they are interrelated in distinctive ways, temporally, spatially and causally.

A philosophy of history need not deal with history, lived or written, as though it were the outcome of the exercise of some fundamental power or powers. And if there were such a power or powers, it still might not be true that the historic future could be known in advance. The historian is no Cassandra. Even when he truly reports the cut of the world, he may be read and heeded—thereby spoiling the aim of any supposed relentless force. And if, as seems to be the case, historic beings all act with some degree of unpredictable freedom, no one can say with surety just what shape history will assume in the future.

There are patterns in history, but they usually embrace only a limited number of beings and run for only a short time. What has great bearing on the items in one pattern may have no or little bearing on those in another. The first world war affected English colonial policy and thereby played some role in determining English attitudes towards Ireland, Canada, and Australia. But it seems to have had little bearing on the development of mathematics in Uruguay. That development would have been substantially what it had been, even if the war had gone the other way, or had never taken place at all. Even a universal conflagration leaves some things but slightly charred. It is rarely that style in poetry or turns in thought in logic are affected by changes in the political or social scene.

A philosophy of history has two primary parts. One concerns itself with the role, presuppositions and activities of the historian and his resultant written history—the topic of the previous book. The other concerns itself with the isolation of the elements out of which objective history is produced, and with the characterization and evaluation of their product. The second is our present concern. We must identify, in the historic world, beings which have one reality and career inside that world and another outside it.

The claim that beings in history have a reality outside it is sometimes thought to entrain the supposition that the categories, methods, activities or adventures of the historic world must echo those of the reality outside. Since history is a domain of time-bound beings, it is held that it must presuppose a reality in which flux is king. Collingwood explicitly makes this assumption. He thinks that no philosophy of history is possible for one who claims that ultimate realities are Aristotelian substances with unchanging essences. He supposes that not until the modern era, when process usurps the place of such substances, is it possible to make a proper place for history. But even a history which encompassed only processes could be grounded in a world of substances. Substances could conceivably together constitute an irreducible historic domain, having its own structure, rationale, values, and course of development. The historic world is not to be characterized as unreal or unintelligible because its existence depends on the presence of beings not in history; the existence of stable and even nontemporal realities does not preclude the autonomous functioning of an historic world. A wife must first be a woman; yet to say that someone is a wife is to say of her something basic and irreducible, and to be ready to deal with her as having a distinctive career, implications, consequences, meanings and values.

There is, as a matter of fact, something absurd in the attempt to take the ultimately real to be events, process, flux. In such a universe there are no beings which can act, persist or be responsible. Artists, workers, ethical men, heroes, and villains would therefore not be part of it. A universe of flux provides no ground for a history in which men act. A juncture of processes of course might yield beings which were not themselves processes, and which could then interact to bring about historic occurrences. In that case the processes, instead of grounding a history, would ground entities which in turn provided a ground for history. On such an account, a history would exist only after the derived beings had come together. Processes can ground a history only through the intermediation of groups of men and nature, both existing outside the historic world. This could conceivably be the case, but the reason for supposing it is cannot be the fact that one had decided to take history seriously. To take history seriously one need take account only of the truth that there is a human realm and a nature, both peopled by substantial beings.

The historic world has its own rationale and its own distinctive features; it is an irreducible world with a characteristic nature and development. The beings on which it depends might conceivably be in an individual mind, be creatures of a cosmic spirit, a destiny or a God. But whether or not this is the case—and I see no evidence that it is—the historic world is a reality, having a distinctive temporal direction, spatial unity, and intelligible career.

The historic world is one product resulting from an interrelating of the basic realities which make up the universe. On the basis of other inquiries I have come to the conclusion that these basic realities are four in number. I have called them Actuality, Ideality, Existence and God (*Modes of Being*, chs. 1–4). Actualities (to speak by and large) are space-time realities, robust, substantial, individual—or derivatives from these; Ideality is the domain of possibility, of the future, of the abstract Good to which all things point; Existence is a divisive power coming to expression in the shape of an extended space, time, and process of becoming; God is an ultimate unity, self-identical, supreme but limited and uncreating. Each of these modes of being is irreducible, permanent, an indestructible element of the universe. Each needs the others in order to be at all, and this need is satisfied in different ways by these others. Each has characters which testify to the demands, presence, and effectiveness of the other modes of being.

In cosmology all four modes of being interplay. Together they constitute a single whole. This has no substantiality or power of its own; it is a pure function of the way in which the various modes of being are together. The four modes interplay with one another in various ways, thereby expressing what they are in and of themselves. Limited combinations of two or more modes are often produced. These combinations constitute *regions*. The regions are like the cosmological whole in which they are located, in that they are produced by an interplay of ultimate modes of being; they are also unlike that whole. Each one of them has a substantiality, power, and rationality of its own.

Even though regions presuppose the coming together of more ultimate realities, they are irreducible, with distinctive structures, vitality, and objective roles. Were the entire cosmos united in such an intensive, intimate way as is characteristic of the regions within it, the cosmos would also be substantial and powerful. But then the various modes of being would have been so fully expressed in an interplay with one another that they would cease to be, thereby self-contradictorily preventing their being together to constitute a cosmos. Regions borrow power and substantiality from their constituents, and can do so only because those constituents still have an independent reality, in and apart from a cosmos of them all together.

Within the cosmos of the four modes, there are then various regions where beings are together more intimately. Outside the regions those beings are cosmologically together in a less intensive way. The more intimate togetherness is characteristic of political wholes, societies and religious institutions. The Hebrews for example think of God uniting with Israel to make a chosen people; the Roman Catholics think of Him uniting with their church to constitute a sacramental reality; Protestants tend to speak of religious symbols or a religious community in a similar vein. God is thought by these various groups to remain at a distance, bridging it occasionally as a concerned or gracious being to constitute with the people, church, symbol, etc., a new, limited region. History is somewhat like such a region. It is the outcome of a juncture of nature and a human realm, the one a large but limited part of Existence, the other itself a sub-region which had already been produced by an interplay of men with a small limited part of Existence.

Nature is a subdivision of Existence. Like Existence, it is dynamic—and spatial and temporal. Every being in it is resistant. Each has a reservoir of energy, a power which comes out in this limited form or that when it interplays with other powers. The beings are also active. There are some philosophers indeed who go so far as to assert that there is nothing so primary as action, and that what we think is stable and constant is but a slowly altering event. But if there were nothing but change or motion there would be nothing to change or move. A world of flux is a world in which nothing does anything, in which nothing is made to come about, where occurrence follows on occurrence relentlessly but nothing is made to be. Quiescence and rest are no less real than change and motion, and all are derivatives from, consequences of the exercise of powers more ultimate than themselves. Rest is the result of an act of self-maintenance against forces which would push or pull a being somewhere else; quiescence is the outcome of an act of self-maintenance in the face of intrusions and conditions imposed on a given state. This does not make them illusory, mere appearances. They are real consequences, just as change and motion are.

Unused power is always present, just beneath the obtrusive phenomena. Each being at each moment has some power in reserve. Each must call upon that power if it is to act and to move, if only to resist others. Were there no such energy one would be unable to distinguish the real from the apparent, the substantial from the phenomenal, the irreducible from the dependent. Were it absent, things would be unable to maintain themselves, to grow, or to change in position, quality or relation. It is this energy which enables them to block, support and withstand others; it is this which enables them to avoid being fully permeated, assimilated or controlled. Without it, things would not even be able to pass away, for before anything passes away it must have the capacity to do so, a potential energy for reacting and yielding to some other. Were there no power in reserve, nothing could act, and nothing could be acted on. There could at most be only a cosmic flickering of lights and shadows, inert and impotent.

In each being there is some unexpressed, unused energy. No one has ever succeeded in peering into it; no one can get over into another's unmanifested side. Still, we do know that each being has energy in reserve. This knowledge we have from the beginning of our careers. If we did not, we would not know that all beings are more than they seem to be. That knowledge is ours because we stand over against the rest of the world, opposing and being opposed by it. In abstraction from such opposition we would be merely co-present in a common field, idle surfaces decorating nothing, tinges in a single continuum of space and time. Opposition serves to keep us apart from one another, to be distinct and effective. No instrument can measure or even report this opposition, for it is one on whose presence the very being and use of the instrument depends. An instrument exists only because it is opposed by others, and this to the same degree that those beings oppose one another. Its operation presupposes the fact of opposition; it can record only specific changes occurring in a world in which beings oppose one another by means of unexpressed energy inside each.

The positivistically-minded thinker denies that there are latent, unexpressed powers. Were he to allow for them he would have to admit that there were realities, or parts of them, which were not knowable by any scientific or empirical device. Still the admission cannot in the end be avoided by him any more than it can be by anyone else. Daily experience and the various sciences pay no attention to positivistic theories, and clearly and vigorously affirm that things have a power to act in ways they do not now exhibit. This all must affirm, if only in order to speak of law-abiding occurrences or to predict what will be. To speak of a law is to make at least an incidental reference to what things might, and therefore can be and do. Whatever laws there are govern the activities of things, dictating that if such and such has occurred, such and such, through the exercise of some power, must thereupon occur. To predict is in effect to say that there is now something not yet manifest which will, and therefore can be. Cut out all reference to potentialities and you deny yourself the right to speak of laws or of predictions, and consequently of dispositions, capacities, abilities, plans, habits, and real existents.

Most physicists and metaphysicians have long ago overcome the temptation to exorcise powers which do not make themselves manifest to some instrument. Both affirm that there is a single whole of energy. It is to this that physicists refer when they speak of conservation laws, of world-lines of force, of a finite universe of space-time-energy, and the like. It is to this that metaphysicians refer when they speak of Existence, prime matter, or the *élan vital*. Since existentialists, nominalists and personalists do not acknowledge a cosmic reservoir of energy, they are forced to people the world with monadic beings, unable to act on one another, to grow or to decay, or even to be related in a common space or time. In the end their theory of monadic beings is reduced to maintaining that oneself as subject exists in and by oneself, hoping somehow that there are others too, to whom one can complain about one's plight. Such consequences show that these philosophers have a philosophy which precludes its being written or communicated. But a philosophic theory which precludes itself from being written or communicated is surely not one that a reflective man can accept. No one can therefore be a reflective existentialist, nominalist or personalist. Only because we already start as beings who exist together, but over against one another, are we able to tell one another how lonely we are.

Some cosmic energy is trapped inside the beings which dot the cosmos. That energy, as in them, has distinctive qualities and modes of functioning. The laws of nature are knotted and gnarled inside the different beings they rule. Those laws come out plain and smooth only when abstraction is made from the specific conditions to which the different beings subject that energy when it is inside their confines. Some of that energy is inside individual men. Some of it is trapped inside societies and institutions, thereby helping mark off the human from other realms. But most of it is untapped by men; it remains outside the realm of human affairs. It there rolls stones down hills, thrusts up oaks, spins the stars, and pulls the planets. Both in the human and the nonhuman sphere, only part of it is actualized at a given moment, and then with a rhythm, a direction, a value, and a use reflecting something of the character of the beings through which it is expressed.

Because they have the power to stand over against the rest of nature, individual men are able to interplay with it. And when they do they acquire new traits—and so does nature. Each man is forced again and again to adjust his private being to the pressures and changes which he publicly undergoes. (He also constantly concerns himself with ends. In addition, he tries to accommodate himself to an ultimate unity, and to deal with other actualities. In these ways he takes account of still other realities in the light of what he intrinsically is and seeks to be.) What is outside him is used as a means for the determination of what he is and will do.

Each man is also in part molded from without. He is at once a function of what he has done and been—and also of the way in which ends have both restrained and helped him, and of the way in which he has been preserved and supported. He is, in short, a creature of many different forces, and he is this as surely as he is one who uses those forces for his own purposes.

A man both uses beings and energy outside him, and is affected by them. When he interplays with them, he and they together constitute a limited *primary region,* a *human realm.* The interplay of that realm with forces outside it yields a *derivative region.* In both the primary and derivative regions, he and others acquire new functions and meanings. In effect this means that he deals with other realities a number of times in different ways. Having, for example, been conditioned by some end inside the human realm so as to constitute a society, he is able to relate himself to the same end in a new way, to make with it a political region in which he, while continuing to be socially involved with the end, functions as a political being. Similarly, his history requires him first to constitute a human realm by interplaying with nature and then to have that realm interplay with the nature that remains so as to produce a new region.

Eight derivative regions—those of tested knowl-

edge, effective virtue, appreciated art, and acceptable worship; public action, organized politics, lived
history, and a divinely sustained institutional religion
—can be profitably distinguished. Together they
make up the world in which men live. In the first
four, men are dominant; in the others they are
sooner or later subjugated by what they encounter.
A perfect equilibrium of men and other powers
cannot apparently be achieved, partly because the
two are not perfectly geared to one another, and
partly because they have unequal strengths.

Tested knowledge, effective virtue, appreciated art
and acceptable worship are derivative regions in
which a man takes account of Actualities, the Ideal,
Existence and God, twice over. When, on the other
hand, he assumes the role of a producer, becomes a
member of a political institution, partakes in history,
or participates in some institutional religion, he is
twice redirected by other Actualities, the Ideal, Existence, and God. He may attend to any one of these
eight regions to the neglect of the others; he may in-
terrelate them in multiple ways. But before he can be
part of any of them, he must have already adjusted
himself to some mode of being so as to constitute a
primary region with it. History comes to be when a primary region, a human realm, constituted by men and
nature, interplays with the nature that still remains
outside that realm.*

---

* The human realm may interplay with other Actualities, with
the Ideal, or with God, and not only with that subdivision of Existence here termed "nature." Technicians and an economic region,
a purposeful and a purposive group, and a dedicated and a
"chosen" religious people will then be produced. Similarly, a
primary region constituted by men and other Actualities (e.g.,
"raw" materials for knowledge and action), one constituted by
men and the Ideal (e.g., a realm of obligation), and one constituted by men and God (e.g., a religion) may interplay with nature
to constitute such derivative regions as an industrial society, a
scientifically tempered moral whole, and a religious community.

By combining derivative regions in which men are dominant with those where they are subjugated, a balance in which men and other factors are on a footing can, at least theoretically, be achieved. A world of rational action, public morality, a cultural history, and a communal religion are the ideal products of such combinations. And they come into being momentarily from time to time. But since we live for the most part in the biased forms, these neutral products should be treated as ideals or paradigms.

Our present concern is with objective history. This demands a prior consideration of the way in which men and nature (and derivatively, man and man, men and state, state and state) interplay to constitute a distinctive primary region. No man lives exclusively in such a region. He may have adjusted himself to any one or to none of the other regions, and may have been molded or unaffected by them. Which of these is the case is of considerable importance to one who would like to know exactly what takes place in history. But they do not affect the question of what man as an historic being is like.

The human realm for each man is, in the beginning, no larger than the region in which he is born; only much later does he occasionally come to see that the human realm contains all men. He is born into a social group—family, village, tribe, community, society (see *Our Public Life*, pp. 22 ff.). From the mo-

---

History is thus only one of many possible regions, and only one of eight derivative regions which result from the interplay of man with a mode of being twice over. I have dealt with five of these derivative regions in previous works. Knowledge is discussed in *Reality*, public action in *Nature and Man*, effective virtue in *Man's Freedom*, organized politics in *Our Public Life*, and art (man dominating, portraying and sensitive to Existence) in *The World of Art* and *Nine Basic Arts*. Two still remain for detailed examination—religion as exhibited in acceptable worship and an institutional religion divinely sustained. A detailed examination of these is the task of a book to follow.

ment he appears in daylight—and from the perspective of custom and law, even before then—he is a member of these. Each group has a distinctive rationale and career. But none is alive, none is an organism; groups are not substances, not individuals. They do, though, have some kind of being. They have consequences as well as implications; they have rights and duties, and often own property, command and make use of power, control and restructure men and their activities. Social groups are to be characterized in ways which are distinct from those appropriate to their parts or their members. A family, community or society may be rich, old or large, while all the members and parts are poor, young and small.

A family, a community, and a society are not readily distinguished one from the other. They do, to be sure, have different types of careers and members, but they also lack well-defined boundaries. They differ usually in size, and primarily in the kind of habituations and directions to which their members are subjected. But there can be large families and small communities which are hard to distinguish, particularly when the former have members who are not related by consanguinity, and the latter have members of that type alone. And there are large communities and small societies which are hard to distinguish, particularly when the former have more

---

* A state is a political institution differing from other institutions, as well as from social groups, primarily in the fact that it is a derivative region governed by law, and that it interplays with similar institutions. Even a tyrannical state is governed by law, differing from other types of states in that it allows one or a few men to stand outside the law, or to make and use it according to individual caprice. A tyrant who had no law to make, use, and control would be a dominating leader of a group or society, not a sovereign in a state. He would dominate a subdued mass of men, not individuals who were acting concordantly in terms of impersonal decrees, carried out impersonally for their presumed peace and prosperity.

In between state and society is the nation. This has the stability

stable, unified, and persistent careers than the latter. Fortunately, for the purpose of determining the nature of the historic, the distinguishing of these different types of groupings is of little moment.

Many historians are concerned with writing about the adventures of states and nations,* either as distinct units or as interacting with one another in diplomacy and war. Part of the reason for this interest is the fact that a good number of these historians have been employed by politically sensitive institutions; but part of it is also due to the historians' interest in large and momentous occurrences. The adventures of states and nations involve great numbers of people, and often in vital ways. Historians consequently tend to focus on derivative regions in which men, individual and institutionalized, and their institutions are interlocked. There is no harm in this provided it is not denied that a human realm and a region of history are then presupposed.†

Men as individuals, in communities and in institutions form enclaves. It is the hope of mankind that these will never be entirely closed off from one another, and that eventually they will all merge into one civilized whole, without denying to the men their rights as individuals, or their roles as constituents of communities and institutions. For men to become fully civilized they must be made into beings who

and often the structure of a state, but its career is that of a society. A nation is a society which preserves its past, and whose members are conscious of or at least live in terms of a common tradition, ideology and aim. Alternatively, it is a state whose laws are part of the life of a people, and which acts primarily to bring about the intensification of common, inherited ways.

† A history of a state is a region produced by the interplay of a derivative region of politics with nature. There are evidently a number of such derivatives, all presupposing the prior achievement of other derivatives. A history of morality, a history of prophetic religion, and a history of discovery and exploration are on a footing with a history of a state. Each of these can be parts of other derivative regions, and so on.

exist together in peace, promoting and benefiting from the arts, commerce, technology, and the sciences.

History, without qualification, is the process of the civilizing of mankind. It is world history, always something more than a collection of stories of independent states and nations, or collations of these. History is mankind expressed over time, inching on in the production of a single civilization where men flourish in peace and justice, fulfilling themselves together as wills, bodies, minds, and persons.

When nature dominates over socialized men, preventing them from living fully or from acting together, it assumes the guise of a brute force, the source of natural disasters. When nature dominates over the bodies of men there is natural tragedy; when nature dominates over their wills she frustrates; when she dominates over their minds she confuses; when she dominates over their persons she is destructive. But benefits can also be traced to nature as operating in independence of men. There is objective history because nature rarely overwhelms men, and then only limited numbers of them and for limited times. History is possible because man is free to make himself one with a part of nature, thereby constituting a human realm, and free to make that realm one with the nature that still remains outside the human realm.

Each man might be said to be a new experiment in the adventure of interplaying with nature and thereby making explicit all that man can publicly be. But then nothing less than the totality of all possible variations in human act and production will tell us what men in the concrete really are. No one of us though has the time, interest or knowledge to study all these variations. In place of them we have fiction, anthropology, sociology—and history. Fiction tells us the kind of consequences any man will produce under conceived and usually dramatic conditions. The playwright and the novelist envisage idealized situations in which a man might conceivably be placed, and then attempt to see what would be the plausible outcomes he might there bring about. In this way they are able to learn what it means for any man to go through paces which none ever actually had gone through, and which none may ever go through. In anthropology one sees across space the different ways in which men express themselves in localized groups; in sociology one sees the nature of the structures and powers to which men are subjected inside a given group, and which dictate some of the roles they then assume. History is interested in man's nature too, but primarily as this has been manifested in an interplay of the human realm and nature.

Man's full being requires that he participate not only in the historic world but in the other seven derivative regions distinguished above. Each of these provides him with an answer to a basic need. Were he able to take advantage of the answers which all of them together provide he would move towards being as excellent as man can be. But what men do instead is to concentrate on living in one of these regions and there finding something like the answers which the others should have provided. They do not, however, ever succeed in cutting themselves off entirely from every region but one, and when they are concentrating on one they mute and transform the kind of answers the others could or did provide. In each region a man assumes a special role which compels him to deal, inside that region, with only analogues of the others. By assuming appropriate roles, he is then enabled to acquire distinctive satisfactions from those analogues.

In each region a man faces demands made by some basic mode of being. If he fails to master other Actualities, he is impotent; if he succeeds he lives as a man, over against and above them. If he fails to meet the demands of the Ideal that he realize it everywhere, he is guilty; if he succeeds he is good. If he fails to meet the demands of the Divine that he assume an attitude of respect towards all that is, he lacks worth; if he succeeds he is saved. If he fails to meet the demands of Existence that he be one with it, he is futile; if he succeeds he is effective. All men fail to meet all these demands. All men are always incomplete. But so far as anyone succeeds, he so far fulfills himself.

In his splendid *Courage to Be* Tillich has underlined some of the main aspects of some of these challenges. He tended to neglect the challenge which Actualities provide, and did not note how a concentration on one demand permits of only a transformed answer to the other challenges. For him the basic and all-inclusive challenge was that offered to man by God; the religious answer to that challenge was apparently thought to be sufficient, requiring no supplement by other answers. But the religious answer is also found inside the others, though in a transformed guise; and conversely, the answer which religion provides takes care of other needs but only so far as they are transformed. To see this it is desirable to note first what men can and cannot do with (a) Actualities, (b) the Ideal, and (c) Existence.

a. Both apart from the historic world and in it, a man takes account of other Actualities on every side of him. They are many and he is one, and as a conse-

quence he is always on the verge of being over-
whelmed by them. They endanger him, reduce him,
show him to be more or less impotent. In the end
they preclude his continuance.

A man lives in a world which eventually spells
death for him. He can meet this challenge for a
while in a double way: he can know, and he can act.
In the one he takes within himself all that lies outside him, and in this sense and to that degree
masters them. In action he goes out to meet them,
subjugates them to his needs and appetities, re-
ducing their threat to his continuance. But his activities in these areas have only a momentary success; in the end he is revealed to be incapable of
withstanding the forces and demands of the rest.
But so far as he succeeds he achieves the dignity of
being a masterful man.

So far as a man concentrates on the task of living
with other Actualities he ignores the demands made
by other modes of being. But he ought to realize an
Ideal; he ought to accommodate himself to a divine
reality; he ought to make himself existentially effective. So far as he does, he will be able to introduce ethical, political, religious, creative and historic values into his life. Only so far as this is possible can he content himself with living as an Actuality with other Actualities. He cannot, to be sure, live
in this way for long, but he can do so for a while.
Sooner or later, though—and usually too soon—his
world is shattered by the imperious demands of
other Actualities. And it is always being intruded
upon by the demands of the Ideal and the possibility of guilt, the demands of the Divine and the
possibility of worthlessness, and the demands of
Existence and the possibility of futility. No man is
ever able to satisfy these other demands fully. All

men are always impotent to some degree. All are, to some degree, guilty, deficient, and futile.

b. Whether or not a man has adjusted himself to the presence of other Actualities, has taken proper account of a primary excellence, or behaved in effective ways, he continues to face the demand of the Ideal that he act so as to realize it everywhere. He is tensed towards the Ideal as the future, and acts at each moment to realize it. So far as he fails he is guilty. Should he succeed in taking into himself the need to realize that Ideal he has virtue and good intent; if he actually succeeds in bringing about a realization of it he is a good man.

The Ideal which a man realizes has a bearing both on individuals in their individuality, and on them as constituting a group. So far as it bears on individuals it is a good which is primarily ethical; so far as it relates to groups it is primarily a political or cultural good. By realizing the Ideal in either way a man escapes the charge of guilt, the one for having failed to live up to his inalienable obligations, the other for having failed to meet obligations that have been ascribed to him. So far as he succeeds in meeting the challenge of the Ideal, he incidentally meets the demands which are made by other modes of being. By living up to the demands of the Ideal a man is enabled to escape the threat of annihilation which other Actualities embody. He does not of course avoid death and impotence, but by allying himself, if only in intent, with an all-encompassing Ideal which gives significance and rational import to all Actualities, he makes himself one who already in a sense controls and masters them, and thus in effect has escaped from the world in which they are exercising their distinctive powers. By substantializing the Ideal as itself all-powerful and good, he can also (with the idealists) avoid the worthlessness which comes from standing away from the most basic excellence; by accepting, with the Kantians, a kingdom of ends as the area in which one's proper life is to be lived, he can also avoid the futility which results from a radical individualism.

Only because a man deals with the Ideal in such a way as to provide some answer to the demands of other modes of being, can he live a full life while remaining an ethical and political being. Were he perfectly good and politically successful he would be able to quiet these other demands. But he can never, as an ethical or political man, do full justice to them. Sooner or later his world is shattered by the insistent demands made by other Actualities; no matter how good he is he must die. And no matter what he does, he cannot avoid the worthlessness that is his because he cannot in fact make himself one with a primary excellence. Nor does his concern for the Ideal permit him to be as effective as he needs be, in art or in history.

By himself a man is unique. Though we may speak of him then as all-important, in and of himself he has no genuine worth. This he can get only by responding to the Divine. It challenges a man to act in the light of itself. If he meets that challenge he is one who assumes an attitude of reverence, or who participates in some organized way in an institution so as to be able to share in or embody a supreme excellence. To the extent that he fails, he is without worth. So far as he succeeds he also incidentally does some justice to the demands posed by other realities. He who lives primarily as a religious man, finds there something like the answers which others obtain in ethics and politics, art and history, knowledge and action. He then sees himself completed in the very dimensions in which he would have been completed had he participated in the other regions. A religion tells him, for example, that though he dies he lives on, that though he is guilty he is forgiven and thus innocent, that though he is inadequate and insignificant he is loved, and therefore important. By his participation in a religion he achieves a worth in terms of which other achievements are to be understood. But a man ought also to survive in this world, meet ethical demands and be effective over the course of time. These demand that he also live and act in nonreligious ways.

Like everyone else the religious man eventually finds himself to be impotent; like the rest he also dies. But he is assured that despite his impotence and death he continues to live on and thus is able to meet the challenge of other Actualities in a new way. Like everyone else the religious man too eventually finds himself unable to do full justice to the demands of the Ideal. Like everyone else he is guilty, at least of sins of omission. He fails to do all he ought. But as a religious man he sees himself to be one who is united with a being who presumably is as excellent as a being can be. He can therefore take himself to be one who has fully satisfied the demands of the Ideal. Despite all failure and wickedness, the religious man consequently supposes himself to be forgiven and in this sense no longer guilty. And finally by virtue of his participation in the power and glory of the Divine the religious man, despite his incompetence and lack of effectiveness in the world, sees himself to have met the challenge of a possible futility.

c. Men meet the challenge of futility directly by engaging in the arts or by participating in history. Should they succeed in living fully in either, they will incidentally and somewhat vicariously overcome their impotence, guilt and worthlessness, as defined by their failure to meet the challenges imposed by other Actualities, by a good that ought to be, and by a divine excellence. These others will of course continue to make their presence felt, with the consequence that the solution which art and history provide will in the end not be entirely satisfactory. But art and history will nevertheless continue to be autonomous regions which provide some answer to man's possible impotence, guilt, and worthlessness.

Only by directly involving himself with other Actualities can a man really manage to survive. But en he enters history he is, by means of an effective ᵤre, able to continue in being long past the end of his natural span. He does this in the course of an effort, through the use of nature, to contribute to the work of mankind over time. If he is successful he achieves a new status, virtue, and worth, and meets in new ways the challenges of futility, guilt, and worthlessness.

Only by submitting to God can a man acquire a true worth, and despite his defects be somehow purged, forgiven, ennobled, made anew through his identification with Him. An analogous worthiness can, however, be acquired by his entering history as a representative man. Though still individually unworthy in a religious sense, he will then be ennobled by becoming part of an historic world.

Though a man can avoid guilt only by doing justice to the Ideal, when he enters history he can adopt an end which has historic relevance, and can so far become an agent for his group, in relation to the Ideal, concerned with a good relevant to others. Just as he is able to achieve a worthiness despite individual failures, so here he is able to live up to a responsibility despite an individual guilt. The soldier may be dissolute and wicked, but as the embodiment of the Ideal carried out in history he, when he does his duty, makes himself one who is an agent doing good on behalf of the entire group.

A man loses worth in history if he does not help make it; he becomes guilty there if he does not live in it; and he becomes impotent there if he fails to adjust himself to it. By using power inside the historic in the role of a representative of other men, he can achieve worth; by using it as an agent he can achieve virtue; and by using it as a cause he can achieve dignity. Historic men function as beings with genuine worth so far as they are representatives of their groups and eventually of mankind. They also deal with prospects which face their own groups, and eventually with a prospect which faces all mankind. And they act on other Actualities in new ways via the groups and the mankind of which they are members. When historic men assume any of these roles, they in effect no longer act as they would have acted had they been fully occupied with religion, politics or action. History can provide a satisfaction only of a transposed and muted form of man's need to be worthwhile, to be virtuous, and to be properly in control. It does not yield the values acquired by living fully in other regions.

Since no man can live fully inside all regions, each must fail to live a *complete* life unless he is able to acquire the very values achieved by those who live up to the demands of other regions. The values can be acquired, however, if a man will make himself a representative of all mankind, firstly by separating himself from his own achievements and making them available to all, and secondly by accepting the achievements of others as his own. A man must at

6

Historic Time

THE WORLDS OF COMMON SENSE, perception, physics, and history are temporal worlds. There are many other temporal worlds besides these, e.g., those of biology, music, and religion. The time in each is distinctive, with its own rhythm, rationale, and nature. The times nevertheless share common features. All spread over an appropraite space; all make it possible for a plurality of beings, despite differences in nature and rates of pulsation, to keep abreast of one another, to be contemporaries for a number of moments; all have within them distinguishable items in a serial order; all allow for a division into a past, a present and a future. Each of the times particularizes these common features in distinctive ways; each consequently has a range, divisions, relations and a being which is different from the others. Some of the times, though no more ultimate and irreducible, are more comprehensive than others. They encompass more items than the others do, as is evident from the fact that they include both the types of occurrence which the other times include, and types of occurrence which these others do not include. The time of the historic world, for example, is a time encompassing both perceived and nonperceived items.

When men interplay with nature they constitute with it the distinctive public time of a human realm. And when, as members of that realm, they combine with the nature that still remains outside the human realm, they constitute with it the distinctive public time of objective history. The time of history is thus less delimited, less specialized, more inclusive than the time of the human realm.

Both the more and less inclusive times allow for the abstraction of times of perception, physics, and the like. An individual man does not live in or through these abstractions. He lives in and through the time of the human realm,* and within the time of history. He also, like all other Actualities, lives in a single natural time. While in that time he also lives in the more restricted, intensive times of history, the human realm, and the subdivisions of these. He cannot of course live in all these equally, any more than he can be equally a part of a small group, a human realm, history, and nature. He lives most fully as a public being when he thinks and acts primarily in terms of historic time and derivatively in terms of the other kinds of time, for historic time is as intensive as but more inclusive than the time of the human realm, and more intensive though less in-

---

* The human realm (and its time) is an objective reality. When that realm is overlaid with conventions, and stretched in some directions and contracted in others, it constitutes the world of common sense. The world of common sense, for example, embraces the stars and the bottom of the ocean; it does not include

clusive than the time of nature. He could think and act as though he belonged only to the human realm or in the nature, but he would then ignore the truth that he is also part of the history of mankind.

The time of history is complex and irregular, encompassing the time of the human realm, within which are more restricted times, characteristic of various groups, institutions, societies, nations, and the like. In each of the times men interact with one another without regard for what is happening elsewhere. The encompassed local times therefore move on in considerable independence of one another. All the encompassed times are specializations of history's time, specializations whose moments differ from case to case in length, structure, content, and pace.

In relativity physics formulae are offered which enable one to connect different local physical times with one another. Not only are there no such formulae available for history, but we are able to observe—as we cannot in physics—the beings which are subject to historic local times, and can know the single historic time which encompasses those local times.

Were the times of the human realm, or of its subdivisions, not localizations of historic time, the world of history would be considerably out of joint. One moment might not yet have elapsed in one area while a number of them had elapsed elsewhere. The times of groups, and the times of the human realm and of nature, are evidently interconnected in history.

In apparent compensation for its range, the observability of its items and its cognizability, historic time is beset with numerous paradoxes. Five of them

the long past and possible future of mankind, which is inseparable from the being of the human realm. From both the human realm and the common-sense world (and from history), perceptual, scientific, and similar strands can be abstracted.

center around the nature of the historic present. 1] The historic present is extended. Though the beginning of it is distant from its end, the entire present occurs as one indivisible unit. 2] The present has three distinctive boundaries, since a. it is still in process, b. is part of a larger present, c. and terminates the past. It therefore has three distinctive magnitudes. 3] In the present there are various concurrent events, some of which are completed earlier than others. 4] Some present occurrences replace others in a sequence, thereby apparently precluding the existence of a single present embracing them all. 5] The present is the last term of the past; but the past has passed away so that there seems to be no series for which the present could be a last term. Each of these paradoxes deserves some attention.

1] All the moments of time are extended. There is a distance between what was and what is to be, a distance which is equal to the magnitude of the present moment. Were the present moment not extended, there would be no time separating the past from the future. But it is impossible to produce an extension out of a plurality of nonextendeds. Since time is extended, since there is a distance between last week and next, the only possible units for time are indivisible extensions, asymmetrically ordered. There are of course subdivisions which one can imagine to be made in any temporal unit, no matter how small that unit be. Those subdivisions will be in an order of before and after one another, but not in a relation of earlier to later. Different moments, though, are in a linear, temporal order, related as earlier and later. The passage of time is the passage of such moments. (Since each man is oriented in a different way, via habit, memory and age, to a common past and future, there is a kind of analogue in time to the incongruous counterparts found in space. No individual is altogether separable from temporal orientation-points in a public world.)

2] (A) The present is a single unit, constituted by a single act, all the parts of which are co-present, through in an order of before and after. It is a present, bounded off from what had been and what will be. If it be true, as I think it is, that there can be no historic present unrelated to a past or a future, a mere historic present must be a fiction. Outside history, though, there would seem to be such unrelated presents. A stone exists in such a present; though it had a past and will have a future, it exists completely here and now. And any act in which one might engage, even while it is related to the present or future, is concrete and vital only as here and now. Though it sounds paradoxical it is necessary therefore to say that a concrete and vital ongoing historic present is only an abstraction.

(B) Every act, while taking place here and now, is, without thought or deliberation, inescapably projected on to nature to constitute a future prospect. This prospect is realized in some specific form in the course of the activity. Unrealized, it defines what parts of a concrete and vital process belong to single ongoing present units; realized it defines what in the dessicated past is relevant to such units.

The present is bounded off from the past, and terminates in the future, to constitute a single, limited, ongoing historic unit. Since the future boundary of that unit is determined by what has been projected forward from the active part of the present, and since it can be projected forward in different ways and for different distances to constitute different prospects, different things might be included in the unit. A skirmish which is part of a battle is distinct from that very skirmish as engaged in idly, pursued as part of a political strategy, or as having the status of a vital incident in a present war. Supplies, for example, which are essential for the conduct of the war, will constitute only the background for an idle skirmish, a skirmish in an isolated battle, or a skirmish which is part of a political maneuvre, but will be integral to the skirmish which is a vital part of the war.

So far as we remain with the skirmish as facing an unrealized prospect, there is no way of determining what will be integral to the skirmish and what will be a background for it. An item which is only possibly integral or is only a possible part of a background is not definitely either. Only the realization of a prospect determines whether a relevant item will be integral or background, and thus whether, e.g., a skirmish is confined to a battle or is part of a war.

(c) The present has a third type of boundary as well; it is closed off from the future but open towards the past. As such it not only determines what is integral and what is background to some limited past occurrence in history, but it offers a point of orientation for the absolute Ideal, enabling this to become an historic ideal, an historic ought-to-be. That historic ought-to-be makes all past occurrences, even those not relevant to the present, into historic occurrences related to that present. Though the past has passed away, and though the present, as the realization of a prospect, is pertinent only to some limited segment of the past, the present, through the action of the ideal, is at the same time made into the terminus of the entire past.

The present both terminates a limited segment of

the past in the guise of a future for that segment, and terminates the entire past in the guise of a value for it. As the first it is a final cause defining a unit of past time; as the second it enables the Ideal to be an Ideal for history. The historian usually takes account only of the former; but he presupposes the latter. There is no incompatibility between them, for the past is reached through them in related ways—the one from the present itself, the other from the Ideal working through the avenue of that present. We will touch upon this question once again in 5 below, and will deal with it in some detail in chapter nine.

3] The difference between various local times is not necessarily solely one of quality; it may involve magnitude. Two battles engaged in by two regiments might begin at the same time, but one may end long after the other. Localized moments may have different lengths. But then how could we be sure that beings at different places are historic contemporaries? The question does not usually occur to us. We usually do not see any problem because we deal with such realities as battles and regiments in terms of some common-sense clock. But no common-sense clock measures the time of history. A common-sense clock is only a mechanism with sharply focused recurrent features used to mark off segments of a common-sense time exterior to it. He who divides a battle into parts determined by such a clock will overlook the plans, the purpose, the acts of both our regiments, and of their war as well.

A battle is no sequence of moments, all of quite small magnitude—say, equal to that which is required for the occurrence of a quantum of physical energy. The battle has a unity occurring in a single moment of historic time. If one battle in one place is not completed when another battle, begun at the same time in some other place, is completed, there would seem to be a lack of concordance between the unit moments. The solution to this difficulty is somewhat similar to that offered in connection with 2 (b) above. The single prospect confronting both battles defines one battle to require a longer span than the other battle does, inside the selfsame present.

4] When we conceptually subdivide a moment into smaller parts, we are in effect denying the reality of the act by which it was constituted, and which now fills out that moment. An incompleted step, with the foot lifted but not yet put down is not yet a step, and thus not a step at all. To subdivide the time so as to allow for a lifted foot which has not yet been put down is to stand outside the moment pertinent to the step. The present can be said to embrace a continuum, but there is no sequential occurrence of elements in that continuum. (Moments follow hard on one another, without interval. There is thus a continuum not only in but of moments. Neither continuum can be subdivided into shorter periods without destroying the moments.)

We do not, of course, step without first lifting a foot. The lifted foot can be photographed; it could be withdrawn; it could be prevented from being put down. A mere lifting of the foot is not now however necessarily part of an act of stepping. Alone, it is outside the act of stepping, bounded off from that act. The fact that, outside the scope of the act of stepping, distinguishable parts of it can be recognized as having occurred in a sequence of distinct moments, and that in fact they do exist in such a way that they make up a sequence in which one replaces the other, only points up the truth that presents of different lengths are possible, and that an occurrence can take place both outside and inside some larger present.

It is impossible to determine whether or not the moments which occur in a sequence of moments are of the same or different magnitudes. Not only is there no way in which we can take any one of these moments and match it against the others, but there is no measure which can be made coincident with one moment without confining it to that moment, thereby precluding its use elsewhere. All we can do is to see if the distinguished items which one moment includes are included in the other including moments, together with additional elements. If a step were dealt with in terms of the space it covers, we could compare two steps (and their moments as well) as larger and smaller, depending on whether the space traversed was larger or smaller. But the two steps will be equally present when they occur, and all of the relevant space will be wholly traversed by each step in its own moment. A larger step covers every portion of the space occupied by a smaller step; it does not first cover the smaller space and then go on to occupy the rest of the space. When we treat a larger single step as first covering a part of the space which the smaller step traverses, we fail to attend to the present of that larger step.

Long-ranged historic occurrences encompass other occurrences within them. The included occurrences are in an order of earlier and later outside the including occurrence. The building of a dam, the waging of a war, the establishment of an empire take years, and require a multiplicity of short-ranged acts and present moments. When we refer to the larger acts and moments we are not making blurred references to a plurality of acts and a sequence of present moments. The included acts occurred in present moments. Though each of these moments is included in a larger present, each also exists on its own. It is thus at once in a relation of a before to an after in a larger present, and of an earlier to a later outside that present.

Since the including historic moment is a present moment, no parts of which are in an order of earlier and later, and since what it includes nevertheless does exist outside it in an order of earlier and later, the shorter spanned items must exist in two distinct ways. He who takes only the larger moment to be real will deny himself the acknowledgment of a real passage of time, covering a number of smaller moments, just as he who takes only smaller moments to be real will have no present in which larger unit acts can occur. How are they to be reconciled?

A possible answer to this question lies in taking a longer unit stretch to be on a higher level than shorter ones. The higher can then be said to provide the lower with an abstract plan or universal which is fractionated by being adopted by the lower. And the higher can in turn be held to adopt the lower as made up of ordered but co-present items. A single realm of history could then be supposed to be the union of the highest possible level with a plurality of absorbed lower level sequences, and of the lowest possible level with a plurality of absorbed higher level structures. A regiments' battles would then be conceived of as being absorbed within an army's war, and the army's war would be conceived of as being fractionated in the regiments' battles. Neither outcome would be taken to be superior in being or value to the other; both would be thought of as abstractions from a more basic history. The time of the war with its absorbed times, and the times of the battles with their fractionated encompassed times, would both be included in a single historic time. History would then have a time which encompassed all three times —the absorbing war, the fractionating battles, and the combination of these two. The times of the war and of the battles would be recognized to be distinct from the time of history. History's time would be seen to be directly fractionated by the time of the war and this in turn would be viewed as being fractionated by the battles; conversely, the war would be directly absorptive of the battles, and the history would be directly absorptive of the war.

This suggested solution has considerable appeal. But it is faced with a number of fatal difficulties. It does not allow the present of the battle and the present of the war to be presents which pass away, for they are said to be absorbed in an unfinished present. Nor does it allow a history to have its own extended present, for this is said to be fractionated by passing smaller presents. It also seems to demand the existence of an infinite hierarchy of histories, each more ultimate than its predecessors. If the absorption and fractionating of war and battles take place in a more basic history, the absorption and fractionating of the history and the war would seem to require still another, more basic history, and so on. And finally, it does not seem to allow that a man can actually be in both a battle and a war. Though a battle might pass away, a man who was in that battle can continue to be in the still ongoing war. No war can be wholly fractionated; no battle can be wholly absorbed; both have their integrity, and a man can live through both.

A better answer is obtained I think if we keep in mind the earlier observation to the effect that a present occurrence has more than one boundary. The included present is in a relation of before and after other distinguishable units in the including present, and is so far not bounded off from them. It does not and cannot pass away as in that including present, except when and as that present does. A present is replaceable by another present only so far as it has its own boundary, and thus only so far as it exists outside an including present.

No matter how long a span an including present may have, even if it embraces the entire career of a people or a nation, no one of the items included in it could be said to pass away. But still it is the case that the people or the nation first did this or that and then did something else. What they did later, replaced, excluded, forced into the past whatever preceded it. And this is possible because the occurrence as present has one boundary, and still another when it is part of a larger present. So far as it is bounded off from the future it is a unit which passes away; so far as its boundary is given by the terminus of the including present it is a part of that including present. The first boundary is determined from within, the second is determined from without.

An occurrence is doubly bounded. As self-bounded, it is past; as bounded either by some future prospect, or by the terminus of an including present having the role of such a prospect, it is part of a continuing history. Each man and each act exists fully inside a self-bounded present which passes away; that present encompasses a genuine historic occurrence, provided only that this also has a place inside a larger whole, where it is related to a past and future.

We always live in an unfinished historic present. We are always completing a subdivision of it, and making this be a genuine present which gives way to another present inside the unfinished present. The completed subdivision is a genuine moment in history, only because it is both self-bounded and bounded at a distance by the terminus of the including present. Every purposed act has a similar structure; the surgeon washes his hands before beginning to cut for the cancer; the washing is a completed act in a surgical operation only so far as it is bounded by the prospective successful cutting. The first movement of a symphony is a completed part of a symphony only so far as it is bounded by the prospective ending of the symphony.

We have here been examining the problem of the relation of a present to another present which includes it. The solution offered is in principle similar to that offered in connection with the problem of the way in which an incomplete occurrence of any magnitude is related to a portion of it which had been completed (2b), and the way in which contemporaries of different magnitudes can be part of one history (3). In all three cases, the future (as something projected, as a shared context, or as the terminus of an including present) defines what is relevant to what precedes that future. Apart from all determinations by a future there would be only a plurality of present ongoings indeterminately related to one another. It requires the realization of the future to determine which part of the plurality constitutes a single occurrence and which functions as background. He who with Hume cuts off the present from the future must with Hume come to the conclusion that the present is made up of atoms all of which are alongside one another, awaiting the act of a mind to bring them together. It would be an error, though, to suppose with Hume that the relation of such atoms could be in an external relation to one another; separated from their future, they are too indeterminately together to be either in an external or an internal relation.*

If there be concurrent events of different magnitudes which do not have a common prospect, the time of the longer event includes the time of the shorter. This means that the shorter battle acquires determinations from the not yet fully actualized terminus of the longer battle. The place, for example, over which the shorter battle was fought may be an area occupied or only a location, depending on whether the longer battle makes use of that place or not.

All of us, as individuals and as members of various groups, live from moment to moment. No matter how we envisage ourselves or what purposes we have in mind, we are governed and unified by possibilities characteristic of our own natures and activities, by possibilities of other longer but concurrent activities, and by possibilities which bound longer including presents. Each of these possibilities has a limited range. A fully determinate past can be only

---

* By approaching an historic present occurrence from outside of history, we are able to identify various components in that occurrence. Inside history those components are in an indeterminate relation to one another, and are consequently indeterminate in themselves. When the occurrence becomes past those components both acquire determinate relations to one another and become determinate in themselves. They then constitute one or many units, depending on whether they are unified or are divided up into foregrounds and backgrounds. In either case an occurrence can be part of a still continuing present. As in that present it will have indeterminate relations to other occurrences which are also part of that longer present. Since those other occurrences may, like it, also be in the past, it would seem that there will be indeterminate relations between and therefore a kind of indeterminacy in those past occurrences. But if all their components are determinate, how could the wholes be indeterminate? And how could there be any indeterminacies in what is past?

The past is wholly determinate because there is a power operating on past occurrences making their remaining indeterminacies fully determinate. The Ideal, operating as an historic ought-to-be through the avenue of the present, is precisely such a power. It turns what in a past occurrence (because of its place in a continuing present) is indeterminately background or essential into

because it is inseparable from one of them. This does not mean that an incompleted present has already been partly completed. If it did, the present would be fractionated into a plurality of successive smaller completed presents. An occurrence for which something future provides a determination is not fully determinate. To be fully determinate it must also be self-determined, i.e. be fully actualized as a single distinct unit.

5] Every present passes away with whatever it then and there encompasses. As already completed, the moment and its content are completely determinate, i.e., given all possible predicates it is the case that every one, in either a positive or a negative form, will characterize the moment and its content. This was not true when the moment and its content were only possible; the possible is indeterminate, general, not altogether specified. Nor was it true of the present. The present is in a process of becoming determinate; it lacks specifications, details, predicates

a determinately relevant cause or obstacle of the present. It bestows determinate positive or negative causal roles on what, from the perspective of some unrealized prospect, is otherwise indeterminate, not yet unified. Two battles which are now over are not yet determinately one single engagement or two, since the war of which they are a part is itself not yet over and cannot therefore determine this. Those battles (even while the war is going on) due to the action of the Ideal, however, are fully determinate, having been turned into causes of what is now taking place. Occurrences outside those battles, though also part of the ongoing war, have the role of determinate obstacles or hindrances of the causal activity of the battles in the war.

An ongoing present leaves undetermined the nature of any being it contains; when past that nature is determined from within, but is undetermined in relationship to other past occurrences, so far as it has a place in the still unfinished present. But due to the operation of the Ideal, all past occurrences are nevertheless completely determinate, turned into beings which contribute positively or negatively, to a present outcome. A causal line may run through only part of a being; a number of beings in an otherwise indeterminate relationship to one another may make up a single causal line in which each has a determinate causal role in a determinate relation to the others.

which it will have when it is ready to pass away.

The present passes away. All of it becomes past. Yet the present was a time when something happened; but nothing can happen in the past. If something could happen in the past, there would be an endless coming to be of the same occurrence, and an endless expenditure of energy. Abraham Lincoln would forever be passing from life to death on April 15th, 1865, and the bullet which killed him would be perpetually flying through the air on April 14th, 1865.

There is nothing substantial in the past, no expenditure of energy, no becoming there. All that the present contained is in it, but in a frozen form. It is the present turned into sheer fact, without give, without any allowance for changes or additions. The unit character of the present, however, is preserved in that past, for the present passes away as a single moment, to make it and its content a unit in a single whole. That departed occurrence can never return, being forever precluded from re-entry into the present by the occurrences in that present. Even a theory of temporal cycles must recognize that one cycle comes after another and that what occurred in a previous cycle remains in that cycle forever. A cyclical theory of time allows only for duplications of previous occurrences and beings; it does not allow for their reappearance except in a form which allows for a distinction between a previous and a subsequent appearance.

There is then nothing in the present which will not be preserved in the past—except the taking place of the present, the expending of energy then, the realizing of possibilities there, and thus the present's existential, extensional time, space, and becoming.

7

The Space of History

HISTORIC TIME needs its own distinctive space. In the space of nature there is room only for the time of nature; in dancing space there is room only for dancing time. Different times have different rhythms, paces and units, and their respective spaces have different intensities, geometries and measures. The point is perhaps most readily seen if one attends first to the features which any space, natural, artifactual, social, or historic, must possess.

Distinct entities may be in contact. If they are not, they are at a distance from one another. That distance is constituted by extended relations, relations which relate relations to one another and are related, in turn, by those relations to other similar relations. If the relations are at once symmetrical (i.e. if like "spouse of" they begin and terminate at both entities) and transitive (i.e. if like "greater than" they relate intermediaries and termini in the same way), they constitute an *area*. Both "coexistent with" and "equals" are at once symmetrical and transitive; when extended they constitute distinctive areas.

An area is *empty* when its relations have minimal intensity; it is *charged* when the intensity is greater than the minimum. It is *occupied* when the intensity is experienceable, i.e. when it offers a recognizable resistance to the senses or to some activity. An occupied area is a *place*. Any conceivable portion of an empty or charged area is a possible place. Since an unoccupied area might be occupied by a body having limits at any part of the area—for example, a body might conceivably be moved any one of an infinite number of distances inside an area—an area evidently embraces an endless number of possible places. The fact is not inconsistent with the existence of minimal spatial magnitudes.

Occupied places are extended. They can never be smaller than the smallest possible particle. Whatever their magnitude they differ from the areas between them only in degree of intensity. Occupied places are extended areas inseparable from less intensive extended ones. Together with those less intensive areas they constitute a *space*. A space is a domain of extended relations embracing occupied places and the areas between them. "Space," though, said Bradley, "is not a mere relation. For any space must consist of extended parts, and these parts clearly are spaces. So that, even if we could take our space as a collection, it would be a collection of solids. The relation would join spaces which would not be mere relations. And hence the collection, if taken as a *mere* interrelation would not be space. We would be brought to the proposition that space is nothing but a relation of spaces. And this proposition contradicts itself."

Bradley supposes that relations cannot relate relations, that relations cannot serve as terms for relations similar to themselves. But this is precisely what an extensional relation is capable of doing. Bradley then goes on to say that space "is evidently more than a relation. It is a thing, or substance, or quality (call it what you please), which is clearly as solid as the parts which it unites. From without, or from within, it is quite as repulsive and as simple as any of its contents. The mere fact that we are driven always to speak of its *parts* should be evidence enough. What could be the *parts* of a relation?" But surely relations can be analyzed out of other relations, and relations may stretch over other relations. If *a* pays *b*, he takes his pen in hand, writes out a check, and then gives the check to *b*. Taking up the pen, writing, and handing the check over are "parts" of the relation of paying. And that relation of paying stretches over the others. The whole of space is an extended relation which is subdivisible into smaller extended relations, all having properties similar to the larger.

If one supposes that space in and of itself is essentially empty, one will be able to speak of it as being occupied by bodies; if, on the other hand, one takes occupied space to be primary, one can speak of empty and charged spaces as derivatives or attenuations of it. Either approach is legitimate. However, we occasionally find that in some occupied places nonspatial features—weight, resistance, change—are discernible. We then properly speak of the place as occupied by some being. Not until we have evidence of nonspatial properties in the place are we warranted in supposing that an occupied area is anything more than an intensification of space.

Space is always divisible in thought, and sometimes

in fact. A moving body successively divides an area into occupied places. But the edge of that body need not coincide with every single point in the area. It would have to so coincide only if motion were continuous. The edge of a moving body need not even coincide with *any* point *in* an area equal to the body's magnitude; if it does not, it moves at maximum speed. But since even discontinuous motion does not skip any points in a traversed area, a moving *body* must touch *every* point in that area. What need not occur is the coincidence by *some* point on the body with *every* single point in the path which is being traversed. A point on a moving body is coincident with only some of the points in the path; but the points it fails to touch are touched by other points of the moving body.

Whether motion is continuous or not, one can always imagine an area being subdivided further. But if there are indivisible unit parts of space (as I think there are), the conceived divisions of it will, after a certain point, be nothing more than divisions of numbers and not divisions of space or of body.

Space is extendable without limit; its magnitude depends on the location of occupied places. Separate these more and more, and the space is extended further and further; bring them closer together, make them into one solid mass, and the space will be contracted, to become nothing more than a single occupied place.

There are many kinds of space. Although the illustrations just given relate to the space of nature, the various definitions have pertinence to spaces distinct from the space of nature, such as the created spaces of architecture, sculpture, painting, play, and dance, the space of sight with its converging rails and its oars seen as broken in water, common-sensical space with its up and down, back and front, right and left, and physical space with its idealized bodies and geometry. These and many others have distinctive properties, dimensions, measures, sizes, units, places. I have discussed some of these elsewhere (see *World of Art*, Chapter 4). Not all are particularly pertinent to the discussion of history. The space of the human realm, however, is relevant, since it is a constituent of the space of history.

The space of the human realm is the space in which we daily live. When we affect that space with social conventions and take it, in practice and belief, to extend to all that is continuous and homogeneous with what is perceived, it becomes the space of the common-sense world. Common-sense space is thus larger than the space of the human realm; it embraces objects outside the human realm, though only so far as they can be related to objects or attitudes in that human realm.

Common-sense space is peopled with substances whose natures we grasp only vaguely, and which we only partly perceive. It includes realities not perceived and others which may never be perceived, though all are in principle perceivable. Common-sense space is occupied by the chair I am now sitting on and by the moon—by anything in fact which is relevant to what I take for granted as I go about my routine tasks. It has a vague and irregular boundary, defining an area much larger than that reached by our individual interests, but not as large as the cosmos.

The space of history is distinguishable from the space of common sense in at least eight ways.

A] *Occupancy:* The world of common sense is a social world, governed by tradition and convention, and organized in accordance with the demands of practical life. Parts of its space are occupied by objects which the experiences, the needs, the language, and the beliefs of a society make conspicuous. Those objects may have a different nature and role in fact than what common sense takes them to have. And they are only a small fraction of all existent objects, and even only a fraction of those which can be encountered.

Common-sense objects are separated from one another by empty spaces. Those spaces may in fact be occupied by objects. But the objects do not happen to be of interest to common sense. The space between buildings, the atmosphere, the cloudless sky, though not actually empty, are empty for common sense. For the unreflecting man space is a single, enduring receptacle, an amorphous region in which its items happen to fit.

In contrast, the space of history is never empty. It is either occupied or charged. A new land or frontier, a discovered wilderness or a desert are, for history, affected by the discoverer. But before they were discovered they had historic reality. An historian may make them the topic of an inquiry and recover for us the nature they had before they had been discovered. America enters the history of western exploration with the voyage of Columbus. But once America was discovered by him, the study of the history of the Indians was possible, and account could be taken of the apparent discovery of America by the Norsemen. We now see the America discovered by Columbus as the outcome of a number of distinct causal lines, and not merely as a new world which Columbus' voyage carved out of a physical part of the globe. From the perspective of familiar present evidence, the discovery by Columbus is history in only one causal line; from that perspective, the adventures of the pre-Columbian Indians and the voyages of the Norsemen are, though historic, not causally significant. But the discovery is in fact the juncture of a number of causal lines, of which the history of the Indians is one. He who views the discovery in this way takes a more inclusive, a more correct, a less provincial approach to the past of America. The past of America, from that perspective, will still contain many causally insignificant historic items, e.g., a suppressed mutiny (if there were one) of the Norse sailors on their first voyage, a minor war between some Indian tribes, and so on. But it will include all of the history of the Indians and Norsemen that is relevant to the nature of America in 1492.

The space of history is no receptacle, as common-sense space is; it is an integral part of history, an extended domain of interrelated historic objects. Changes in the nature, being, role and relationship of those objects affect the structure and thus the nature of the space of history. We take some cognizance of this fact when we acknowledge that the Greek city-state has no counterpart today either in our cities or in our states. The friends of Socrates lived in one space; the Greeks today live in quite another. No restoration of the Agora will ever recover the old space, for this exists only when and where a now departed society does.

B] *Structure:* Common-sense men are realists, substantialists, but without a clear idea of what it is towards which they are directed. Their space is oriented primarily towards external things. The foreground of that space is rather sharply distinguished from its background, which suddenly stops to give the limits of their common-sense world. In the foreground there are curves and bumps, but the background seems, on the whole, to be smooth and flat.

Because the space of common sense is only partly filled, it is a space which is essentially discontinuous, whose occupants are so many separated mounds in an empty plain. Each occupant intensifies and thereby curves the space in which it is. When then it is said that common-sense space is Euclidean what is meant apparently is that its empty space is so. Its occupied space is evidently non-Euclidean, and the combination of the occupied regions and the empty ones is a mixture of the two.

In contrast, the space of history is continuous, and charged and occupied throughout. But the intensifications characteristic of the occupied portions are discontinuous; a spatial field, with a distinctive character and role, connects the various occupied portions. Depending as it does on the nature and activity of the objects in it, the structure of historic space varies considerably from place to place, and from time to time. There are sudden shifts in emphasis and stress, quick jumps in importance from place to place in that historic space.

It is questionable whether it is appropriate to speak of historic space as having a geometry. It can be said to have a metric, but one not measurable by rods or other instruments. An order sent down the chain of command is usually carried by a messenger, or transmitted by signals, telephones, and so on. Measured in miles, the distance from the sender to recipient may be very great; yet the time taken may be very short. Conversely, though the two may be quite close, perhaps a room away in the Pentagon, the message may take days to go from one to the other. The spatial distance in the former is shorter than in the latter. However, we cannot determine how short this is until we have determined the metric for the space (see p. 170 ff.).

c] *Pivots:* Common-sense space is a field of many privileged positions in terms of which the primary relations to the rest are to be understood. There are many pivotal points, central places in it, at which interest, action, and meaning converge and from which they depart. The space is oriented in each member of the society in one way, and in its leaders, institutions, and cherished places in other ways.

As a rule, a leader in a society stands out as a being towards which and from which actions are directed. No matter where the leader is he is at the center, and others are at some distance, facing him no matter in what direction he or they happen to be looking, providing they are in some consonance with him. On the other hand a conspirator may look him in the eye but be directed away from him, while he may face another and not take account of him.

Institutions offer stable organized patterns of behavior. Much of the life of a community is geared in terms of the rhythms and location of church and court, throne and granary. Though these may be on the periphery of the society in physical space, they are points around which all else clusters. Washington is a tourist centre, but it is not as close as Denver is to the geographical centre of the United States.

A society often has sacred groves and places, or, failing these, shrines, monuments, and other signal spots towards which one must behave in certain ways. They are foci in times of stress and on holidays. Though a common-sense man is often unreflective, and functions with insufficient understanding of himself or his society, he makes constant use of such pivots. Everything in his world is humanized, even the physical things and the institutions towards which he may direct himself or in terms of which he may live. But some of these pivotal points, though they have a bearing on the destiny of man, are neither known nor attended to in history. In history, too, a mass of men may provide a pivotal point in terms of which subsequent events can be explained and clarified. Usually such a point is not recognized by the people for whom it so functions, or who constitute it. A town may slowly decay and its population vanish, almost fade away without anyone apparently knowing why, how, or even that any change had occurred; yet the event may be vital for the understanding of a good deal of history.

D] *Dimensions:* Up and down, right and left, backwards and forwards are the three dimensions of common-sense space, radiating out from each of its members. The dimensions continue to and through objects, aligning them in the different dimensions. As a rule the different directions in a given dimension have unequal importance, in part because a movement towards a focal point has a different rate and import from one which moves from that point. Actions in symmetrical space are often asymmetrical in value and rhythm.

"Right" and "left," "up" and "down," "back" and "front" have a somewhat different meaning in history from what they have in common sense. Front and back in history are temporarily tinged dimensions, referring to what will be and what had been; they are determined not by a man's body, but by his actions. When we try to think of the commonsensical or historic past or future, we usually continue the lines leading towards a common-sense front or back; but unless we are bewildered by our own devices, we will not suppose that we are thereby turning time into space, or that the space of common sense has become the space of history. Front and back characterize a co-present area of common-sense space, but what is towards the front in history is what is to be, and what is towards the back is what had been. Nor are up and down in history determined by the head and the feet, as is the case with common sense. They refer to the relation men have to an area over which they can move. When, as in modern times, men take to the sky, that sky, though overhead, is "down" with respect to the men who make use of it. Finally, there are, strictly speaking, no rights or lefts in history, except so far as they have a differential use. Caesar, to be sure, had a right and a left arm, whether he used them in different ways or not, but this is a common-sense truth or one in physiology, not one in history. It is a fact of history though that Caesar went from North to South across the Rubicon, and that the Adriatic was on his left. Apart from their role in the historic occurrence, or their relation to some other historic occurrence in which similar differentiations are significant, the different directions are indistinguishable. The idea is a little startling at first because we are so accustomed to think of all things in common-sense terms, because we relate undifferentiated features of historic occurrences to others in ways which require a differentiation, and because the historian may add such differentiations to an historic fact to make his account more familiar or vivid.

Although the men and things, with which history is concerned, occupy volumes, there is no voluminous space in the historic past. Julius Caesar does not now take up any room. To do so would require action, insistence on his part. That he once displaced a volume of air is undoubtedly correct, but that is not a fact of history. That he and Brutus, he and the Rubicon, he and his army were at various spatial distances from one another is true, but the distances are now only relations between facts, and the beings in which they terminate are now only determinate, dessicated residuua of what once had been dynamic and voluminous.

E] *Environment:* There is a large area outside common-sense space. This may be occupied by objects, and some of those objects may not be perceived. There are many occurrences in natural space of which common sense knows nothing; but they and their areas are related to what common sense knows. Though, as was indicated before, it is an error to suppose that we could perceive stars which are millions of light years in the past, it surely is the case that there are heavenly bodies which are at a distance from us. Common-sense space is a demarcated part of a wider space which serves as the background and the source of the material out of which common sense forges its characteristic space.

There is also an area outside the space of history. History indeed has being only because there is such an outside area. But that area is not a background for history, nor does it provide an environment for it. The occurrences in history have backgrounds and environments; history itself does not. The historic world is completely self-enclosed, though it depends for its being and power on nonhistoric realities.

F] *Relation:* We live in common-sense space. It relates us to whatever else there be in our society. We can make that space an object. That is what sociologists do. To follow them is to take a first step in the

acknowledgment of an historic space. A society con-
tributes to a history in the making, but the space
and events in it do not have an historic import until
they have both passed away or have been related to
subsequent ones in a distinctive historic way. Historic
space is a past common-sense space related to predecessors and successors. These predecessors and successors make any momentary state of common-sense
space one term in a historic sequence of states.

   Out society today had predecessors and will have
successors, but this fact common sense neither knows
nor allows. The successive common-sense spaces are
linked in an objective history. Since history takes
account of some items which common sense ignores
—e.g., the causes of famine and war, the nature of
diplomacy, the struggle for power, the self-deception
and errors of scholars, the art of forgery and the like
—as well as of what common sense includes, history of course offers us much more than a story of
the way in which social worlds and their spaces are
related in time.

g] *Reality:*   Common-sense space is a real space,
though muddled and overlaid with convention, and
even superstition and error. To know space as it objectively is, it must be freed from the execrescences
that common sense inevitably introduces. One must
distill out of common-sense space a number of
strands which are there intertwined and then, after
having freed these from extraneous elements, combine them into a single unity. The result will be no
mere fiction, but an icon, a representation of a non-
conventionalized objective space. It will be the space
of common sense, purged, freed from the limitations
which had been imposed on it by society.

   In contrast, historic space presupposes realities

which are more ultimate than it is. One of these is the space of nature. (This is not a physical space; physical space is a matter of formulae, a mere geometry.) Historic space is the product of the interplay of the space of nature with the space of the human realm, fragmented and qualified at every moment by particular societies. It is spread out over an area larger than that which concerns perception or even common sense. And it constantly pulsates, expands, and contracts. It takes in regions which are not perceivable and others which common sense may take to be irrelevant, such as lands lost long ago. But it does not reach to the limits of the cosmos, nor does it encompass all the beings that exist, for what does not impinge on human affairs does not occur inside it.

H] *Distance:* History's space is a humanized one. Distances in it have a distinctive meaning. Two distances in historic space may be found to be equal in length when abstracted from that space and then measured by the eye, by walking, or by a rigid bar. But they may be unequal when measured in terms of the number of distinct historic efforts that must be taken to bridge them, or when measured in terms of the relevance their termini have to what men historically are, desire or do. One of the distances may separate a man from an object in which he has little or no interest, while the other may terminate in a destination anxiously sought. A neglected road might cover one distance, a well-travelled road another. One of the distances might go through a swamp or a jungle, while the other might be measured along a road, a bridge or a tunnel. Both distances might be members of a family of somewhat similar and equal distances, or each might offer a distinctive distance between two beings, pushing everything not traversed by it into an indifferent background.

We might sometimes get the same numerical result when we measure a distance in historic space and when we measure it in abstraction from that space. But the result will have a different meaning in the two cases. Only in the former is the meaning inseparable from the nature of the related beings, and the relations they have to one another. Though it makes sense to say that the army is six miles from the border, it is one thing for the distance to be six miles from a friendly border and another thing for it to be six miles from an enemy border. And it is still another thing for the six miles to separate two friendly armies and not two enemy ones. In these different cases the six miles are overlaid with different meanings.

An historic spatial distance relates contemporary beings. So far as the beings act in consonance with respect to some common objective there is no distance between them—even if they are separated by a continent. Two regiments, though widely separated in natural space, are at no distance from one another if they function harmoniously as parts of a single drive. Each of the regiments is itself spread out over a terrain, but this fact is historically relevant only so far as there are minor objectives to be thereby reached, or if there is some lack of concordance among the platoons, squads, or soldiers, failures in communications, supplies, replacements, and the like. A unit measure for their historic spatial distance is any single act which adjusts them with respect to a common objective. A communication, which converts them into beings that act concordantly with respect to a common objective, provides a unit measure of the spread between them.

Regiments, separated from one another in natural space, usually are discrepant in act and achievement. Since the regiments start from different positions, they also inevitably confront different intermediary objectives. Those objectives serve to separate the regiments from their common objective and make evident that the regiments are discrepant in nature, intent or act. Were both regiments occupied with the same objective, and were there no intermediaries between themselves and that objective, the two regiments would be integrated parts of a single unit. Any reference to their spatial distance would then relate only to an abstract aspect of the single unit they together constitute. If we look at the regiments in terms of a final victory they will, so far as they mesh in act and result, be in the same place. They will be separate and independent, at a distance from one another, only so far as they are concerned with different intermediaries or are discrepant with respect to the final objective.

Could we all reach an ideal historic outcome there would so far be no historic spatial distance between us. But history will nevertheless go on if we then diversely struggle with nature in order to reinstate the ideal terminus moment after moment. Since the final objective, if perpetually realized by distinctive acts on the part of independent beings, has the role of a prospect only a single temporal unit away, it will so far be the common objective of beings at a unit spatial distance from one another.

An action which converts a singular opportunity into a shared result offers a unit of temporal distance. It measures the step from a final intermediary to a common objective. Since beings without a common objective are not in a common historic space, and since harmonized beings with a common objective are not distant from one another in that space, there can evidently be spatial distances in an historically relevant space only because beings are not concordant, or because concordant beings are at a temporal distance from their common objective. In the latter case, the dependence of space on time is a consequence of the fact that beings which engage in distinct acts are so far distinct beings, necessarily separated in space because separated with reference to a common objective in time. The dependency does not follow from the fact that it usually takes more than one unit of time to transmit something from one spatial point to another. Two harmonized actions having the same objective are in effect the action of one historic being, no matter how these actions be named or generated; two objectives reached by single acts are in effect the objectives of distinct entities, no matter how closely packed together these entities are.

The space of history, like the space of common sense, embraces the human realm and nature. In the common-sense space, the space of the human realm and that of nature are not united; they are merely brought together through perception, interest, and belief. The space of history, in contrast, is a single unitary space, produced through a synthesis of the space of the human realm with the space of an otherwise unhumanized nature. We can take it to be the product of a synthesis of common-sense space with a natural space beyond it, providing we recognize that the synthesis of these two is accompanied by a synthesis of the space of the human realm and the space of nature, which otherwise would be merely together in the common-sense space.

Depending on whether men are acting as one or as many with reference to a common objective they, through concern, action, status, role, and intention, subdivide space into points or areas. An area varies in structure and range depending on the degree of discrepancy men exhibit in their actions. It has no distinctive nature of its own. Without value or nature, it provides a field where a plurality of beings can be found to act somewhat out of gear with reference to the same objective.

Animals sometimes form classes ruled by powers outside them; like men they are members of teleologically governed groups. These groups may sometimes be so splendidly organized and integrated that the members of them, though working in harmony for long periods, have no history. An anthill is just a spatial point without a history because the ants realize a common outcome by carrying out their interdependent roles in excellently coordinated ways. In contrast, by their oppositional intentions and acts, fighting stags constitute an area having a distinctive magnitude, nature and structure. Since that area does not itself interplay ·with others, it, unlike a society or nation, is unable to constitute a history. History depends on the existence of effective realities interacting with one another and with an external nature.

If, as is claimed by evolutionists, various groups of animals are affiliated; if secondly, as the orthogenetic biologists go on to maintain, the groups are produced through the action of powers outside the beings and their groups; and if, finally, the groups have common objectives, it can be said that the biological world is so far an historic one. This still would not mean that biology was history, for, as was observed earlier, though living beings might be in history, it is the intent of biology to do nothing more than isolate recurrent patterns and far-reaching laws, whereas history seeks to date, relate and trace the singular movements of particulars.

Since we have no evidence that groups in nature share common objectives, we have no warrant for supposing that there are historic routes in nature travelled concurrently by a number of different kinds of animals. The most we have a right to suppose is that there can be a history for a number of somewhat discordant animals of a given group, and then only so far as they face the same objective, such as the preservation of the colony or nest. But animals have no traditions; they do not preserve or take account of their distinctive pasts. If then there were a history for animals in a given group, it would cover only a single generation, after which another history, not altogether identical with but somewhat similar to the previous one, would take place, and so on.

Men, apart from history, help constitute the distinctive space of the human realm. And they occupy what they help make. This space differs from the spaces available to other beings in a number of ways. Firstly, men affiliate with one another as other kinds of beings do not. Human memories, conventions, associations, and interests are unlike those which other beings manifest. Some of man's affiliations are sustained by training, habit, convention, and above all by manners and language, thereby enabling him to make connections with beings quite distinct from himself in temper and place.

Also, men are tradition laden. What they do is persistently affected not merely by what they themselves have done before, but by what their predecessors have done. The past is effectively present in the lives of men, a past which they have not themselves experienced. Since the groups men form are themselves unities, governed by such common objectives as human welfare, peace, and prosperity, the groups can be elements in a history. And since the objectives which are common to a group can be adopted by individual men, the men can become representatives or agents of the group, and may thereby control the activities of the group. Each of these facts make common-sense space and the space of the human realm, and therefore history, considerably different from any other, including that which is characteristic of a number of animals working in separate ways to realize a common end.

Looked at in terms of common objectives which individuals or groups of them pursue, concordant individuals (or groups) are indistinguishable one from the other. The principle of indiscernibles, expressed by Leibniz, here finds a new application. Beings which are not different in feature are not, this principle affirms, different in being. The principle holds of men and groups in history, but only so far as these are concordant with respect to the same objective. Men (and groups), however, do differ from one another in the way they evaluate common prospects. They are so far distinct and at a distance. Alike so far as they are oriented towards the same objective, they differ in the way in which they evaluate and privately utilize what they pursue in common. They become incongruous counterparts, for though they face a common good, they give it different weights in their different economies.

So far as men are in history, they exist in a distinctive, spatially extended realm. But men are never part of history in their full substantiality. Their unrealized potentialities are not part of history; history encompasses only what they manifest. Their actions, too, start from and are sustained by what has not yet come into history. And they have other interests and activities that are carried on outside the historic context. Not only do men attend to mathematics and the various sciences, but they have religious, ethical, and aesthetic concerns which either undercut or abstract from historic contexts and involve the exercise of powers not used in history.

Historic space is occupied by affiliated men and groups whose distances from one another are a function of the degree of disaccord they exhibit when pursuing a common objective. Though dependent for its being on the union of the space of the human realm and the space of nature, history's space has an objective being and irreducible reality of its own. It is through this space that the time and causation of history run their course.

8

Historic Causation

ENERGY MUST BE EXPENDED if there is to be action, movement, change. Energy must also be expended if things are to remain as they had been. Quiescence, rest, continuance are states achieved in the face of forces which would otherwise compel changes in position, quality, nature or being. Expenditure of energy in the latter cases is obviously not observed; only reflection on the way in which beings are able to maintain themselves unaltered for a period of time leads us to say of them that they must expend energy in order to continue as before.

Strictly speaking, we do not observe that energy is expended when bodies act and change. We come to know of the fact only as a result of reflection on the causes and necessities of motion and change. We do, to be sure, see that beings are active, moving, changing, that they come to be and pass away, that they remain unaltered or at rest. But what kind of "seeing" is this? Do we perceive change or rest? I think we do. The fact is usually overlooked because three types of perception are not distinguished. These types differ from one another in temporal span, and consequently in what they comprehend. All of them involve the use of sensed content; all involve judgment; all refer to some encountered occurrence. (a) One type of perception precludes any knowledge of change or motion; it occupies only a single moment. (b) Another type allows for an experience of change and motion, but not for a knowledge of it. Here a number of perceptions are held together by memory and expectation. (c) A third type allows for the encounter and knowledge of changes and motions, continuities and rests. In all three a subject or subjects and a meaning are distinguished, and then united by us in a judgment rooted in content lying outside that judgment. The perceived, though constituted by us, is in all three cases objective, inseparable from an externally existing reality.

A]   A past perceiver can no longer act; a future perceiver is not yet in a position to act. Perception must take place in the present, and the perceiver and the perceived must be there too. The perceiver exists while he perceives; the perceived is the terminus of his act. He cannot look into the past, since this has passed away; he cannot look into the future for that does not yet exist. He and the perceived are copresent, and both are in the present. This does not mean that either is entirely sundered from the past or the future. Each of us perceives as a man of habit and training, and what we perceive is the terminus not only of the senses but of beliefs, tensions, attitudes. These, though issuing out of the past and relating to the future, are nevertheless perceptually effective here and now, in the present moment of perception. And they need not distort the nature of what is encountered. Since the reality in which the perception terminates is itself an outcome of past adventures, and implicates new realities in the future, the perceiver, when well-adjusted to the world, is enabled through his habits and attitudes to act in accord with the nature and promise of the object at which his perception terminates.

The moment in which perceiver and perceived are together is extended. Within that extended moment items related as before and after can be distinguished. If then by perception of change and motion one means a sensed and judged replacement of one quality or relation by another, there can be no perception of change or motion in a moment. Change and motion demand replacement of one content by another, and this requires at least two moments.

Perceptual content is rarely homogeneous. Usually qualities and sets of relations which are present in the beginning of a moment are different from those present at the end. But whether they are the same or different, there is no process of alteration, no motion to be found within it. In a perceptual moment, as Whitehead observed, the flying arrow does not move. Nor does it change in quality, shape, magnitude, or in any other way. But, as Whitehead did not seem to allow, the arrow does survive the moment in which it is perceived. Our perception of it does not exhaust it. Perception exhausts only the object as then and there momentarily perceived.

The flying arrow survives the present perceptual moment, and can be known to survive it in at least five ways. Like all objects, firstly, it is an irregularly pulsating thing, and remains steady in some respects while it alters in others. And some of the respects in which it remains steady continue to be moment after moment—a truth of course which cannot be known except so far as we make use of grounded expectations and thus move out of the reach of the perceptual moment. Secondly, the arrow has potentialities. It can be bent and broken; it can be let fly; it can be heated, coated, stepped on, let drop, and so on. When we perceive it we have a dim awareness of its potentialities, for our perception is rooted in the object perceived, terminating in its potentialities. Thirdly, the arrow is encountered as a common-sense object, as an entity in a social context, exhibiting some features which are perceived, others which are cognized, and still others which are open to evaluation or have a reference to possible use. Though the arrow may be perceived to be in some position or state for only a moment, the arrow as an object of common sense continues to be and to function. Fourthly, we all have a kind of experience which transcends the reach not only of perception but of common sense. At every moment we have a dim awareness of a powerful dynamic reality lying outside the confines of our daily world. That reality spreads far beyond the borders of the arrow, but it is not altogether separated from the arrow; it has a degree of concentration at the arrow greater than it has outside the arrow's borders. The arrow is able to survive the present because the power which is in it is inseparable from power outside it. When we encounter the arrow we have a faint apprehension of the substantial, irreducible existence of which the arrow in and of itself is a part, and which has a career in no way confined to what is momentarily discerned in perception. Finally, we come to know the arrow in and of itself through the help of a speculative philosophic system, though of course then only as illustrating universally applicable categories and principles. Though the arrow is not perceived to move or change in the present it is nevertheless known speculatively, and in other ways, to be more than a momentary perceived object.

B]   It is rare for us merely to perceive. It is rarer still for us to engage in a series of mere perceptions. What usually occurs is that we have an experience, in which the subject or experiencer and the content or experienced are terminal points, each having reference to the other. Perceptions individually or in a series are analytic subdivisions of the experience, and depend for their isolation on a separation by the experiencer of himself from the experienced, and the subsequent introduction of an act of judgment, itself an analytic part of a moment of experience.

We know that there are changes and motions, that things come to be and pass away. But we cannot know these so long as we remain confined within a single perceptual moment. We can see a color change or a dog run, can hear a change in timbre and pitch, can feel a rough surface give way to a smooth one. Such knowledge involves a passage of time in which content and moments are replaced by others. And there is always some memory of what had been and some expectation of what is to be. The sequence of moments and their sensed contents are held together in the perceiver, and he as a consequence finds himself confronting central, focal, and vivid content, over against a peripheral dim background which is acknowledged to have been, or to be capable of becoming focal. The object is seen here as that which had been there and which can be further on. It is experienced as having one quality against some other faintly remembered and expected qualities.

We experience when we perceive and also when we do not. If we perceive as well as experience we live in two present moments. Each of the perceptions takes up atomic moments which have smaller spans than the experience. As caught within the experience they are all co-present; as products of genuine acts of judgment they occur in sequence, one passing away with the coming to be of another. The perceptions which our experience encompasses are all had as having an orientation outside the experience and, so far, as having careers other than what they have in the experience. We are therefore able to know that we had perceived something, or that we are about to perceive something, while we remain within the confines of a present experience.

c] We experience change and motion. But we also perceive it. The experience can itself be made the object of a perception; it may have perceptions as parts. There are perceptions, and thus encounters, judgments, and present moments which encompass experiences having perceptions as parts. In the encompassing perceptions various experienced, remembered, and expected qualities and positions are given a place alongside focal content.

We perceive an object as in the process of moving from one state to another because we face experienced, remembered, and expected parts of the perception in terms of a focal area. The focal area is imposed by us on them as a norm, and we then note how it is effectively rejected on one side and accommodated on the other. Our perception of change and motion is thus the outcome of an attempt to make a focal area fill out an experienced region. An experienced faded-color is perceived as that which had been brighter or might become lighter. This perception differs from an experience of change and motion in the fact that it depends on an effort to reconstitute an experience, an effort which is defeated by the experience itself.

A perceptual object does not persist. Its career is exhausted in the moment in which it is encountered. It has no other being than what it is perceived to be. From it we can learn nothing about its neighbors, nothing about its causes, influences, purposes or potentialities. But it is inseparable from an adumbrated content which merges into a more substantial reality, having a dynamics distinct from that of the perceptual object.

A perceptual object is a facet of a common-sense object, where it is merged in a somewhat inchoate manner with other facets. A scientific object is one of those other facets. When we seek to express the common-sense object in formal terms, so as to have it through and through cognizable and law-abiding, we focus on the scientific object, designing and isolating it by means of our formulae and concepts. A realm of scientific objects, strictly speaking, has no vital ongoing in it. There is nothing there but logical relations, laws relating antecedents and consequents.

A common-sense object is not always perceived. But it is in principle always perceivable. Sometimes experienced, it is also in principle always experienceable. Substantial, it occupies its own kind of space, goes through its own time, and exhibits its own dynamics. We confront it as men who have been trained in act and speech to signalize certain features of it, to impose certain interpretations on it, and to use it in special ways and on special occasions.

The common-sense world, like the common-sense men who occupy it and know it, is overlaid with interpretations, stresses, and meanings which reflect the values and interests of some society. It is a world in which historic and other types of causality are rooted. Different societies approach its objects in terms of different languages, concepts, categories, habits and attitudes, dictating what is to be seen and used. An arrow for an Indian has quite a different common-sense status, nature, and meaning than it has for a member of our culture. For the one it is an instrument, for the other a sign or a bit of historic evidence.

As common-sense men we find ourselves making a difference to other things, and rather readily suppose that the same kind of causality is in operation everywhere. Denied this supposition we would have to deny the finality of our common-sense world and thus ourselves as common-sense men, or would have to hold that we are odd creatures who not only function as unique causal agents but who misconstrue the world in terms appropriate only to ourselves. So long as we remain common-sense men we deal with what we confront in familiar causal terms. We know no way in which to avoid this except by ceasing to be our daily selves.

Common-sense causality involves the interplay of individuals, organizations, and a nature lying beyond both. The causality is the locus of scientific laws, perceptual occurrences and the like, embracing the individuals, organizations, and the nature beyond these, as they interact to constitute a human realm. We will understand that causality better I think if we first take account of the causality which is of interest to law, social life, and public action.

Legal causality has to do with the legally defined source of a liability. This need not be a power which in fact brought about some damage. As is most evident in Federal employment liability cases, the determination of the cause is one with the determination of liability, and the latter may refer to nothing other than a socially acceptable determination of where the liability should be ascribed, regardless of fault. The law usually looks to what is nonnormal to account for what is not desirable. The nonnormal occurrence may be better or worse than what usually takes place. Sometimes it is the advantaged individual or institution which is made to assume the liability, on the good grounds that this advantage is something owing to the society and therefore necessarily entails an attribution of liability greater than that characteristic of those not advantaged. Sometimes, particularly when the disadvantaged is a source of undesirable activities, it is the disadvantaged who is taken to be liable. In either case, the determination of liability is usually conditioned by the availability of the recompense, and the attitude of the society regarding the justice of making the attribution of liability fall on those who are without causal power or without genuine fault in the situation.

Similar accreditations occur in societies. For them the cause of any occurrence, good or bad, is that which is believed to make a difference to the well-being of the members. There is here no consideration of what would be a most effective and acceptable way of attributing liability or rewardability, nor is there a concern, as is usually the case in the law, with what can be objectively ascertained to have acted in ways relevant to the damage sustained. In social causality, one normally rests with what is commonly believed to be a cause of the promotion or destruction of man's well-being.

There is also an institutional causality, characteristic of institutions as small as clubs and as large as states, in which reference is made to those objectively ascertainable modes of action of the institution which will enable it to operate effectively. An individual member of the institution, any institution outside it, and the world beyond may be the source of the energy transforming the institution into one which is able to function, but these will have no institutional causal power until they become transformed into agents for the institution. As outside the institution's control they have a noninstitutionalized power; as responsible for changes in the career of the institution they can then become elements in an objective history. Institutional causality relates to the way in which the institution's functions are understood in terms of some part of the institution. There is no institutional causality when the members of a corporation are wiped out by some disaster; there is no institutional causality when a sudden demand for a product springs up. But there is institutional causality when, in the attempt to meet the demand, one overworks the men, improves efficiency, hires more men or buys more machinery.

There is also a cultural causality in which a reference is made by men in the culture to what is believed to make a difference to basic values, as well as to what in fact does make such a difference. Cultures—or, to speak with some historians, civilizations —ranging from groups related by habit and language to those which have a common purpose, have thus something of the features of a society and of an institution. Like the former they are governed by judgments which reflect beliefs rather than facts; like the latter they are occupied with the facts which determine what is actually effective in bringing about a desired or undesired result. In a culture one looks for what makes a difference to the members and to the culture as a whole. Beliefs are important, as they are in society, because one also lives inside the culture; objective facts are important, as they are in institutions, because the culture is recognized to have an objective status, outside the particular members which constitute it.

In all these kinds of causality, some antecedent is relevant to some outcome. All of them together make up that basic but muddled world in which we daily live. There is no question in any of them of a demonstrated source of the energy which in fact produces an effect. The dynamics is one whose paths are defined by the beliefs, needs, and structure which relate some antecedent happening to some outcome.

Our daily world is crisscrossed with all these different types of causality, and allows for the analysis of them severally and together in the formal terms of science, the judgmental terms of perception, the creative terms of events, and the evaluational terms of an ideal. History is the locus of all these causalities when these have been interlocked with the causality characteristic of nature.

The causality of nature is distinct from the causality of interest to law, society, institutions, and cultures. Law ignores nature except when it speaks of "acts of God"; it sees individual men only as potential, publicly effective agents. Society ignores nature except as a source of nourishment, energy, and possible disaster, and deals with the individual as a mere unit or in some role. Institutions and institutional studies ignore nature except as a background or as a source of "raw" material; they have no place for the individual except as a part. Cultures ignore nature except as a condition for success or failure; they have no place for the individual except as the ultimate being to be benefited, or as a signal source of some basic advance or loss. The world of history, however, is one in which legal orders, societies, institutions, and cultural fragments all play a role, and which redefines the role and promise of individuals and nature.

Historic causality embraces what in fact is affected by tradition and convention; it also encompasses impersonal forces. At every moment, history unites the human realm and nature to give us a new reality. The human realm and nature together yield a distinctive historic cause which is freshly expressed in an historic process of causation, terminating in an historic effect.

Men and nature have one role in history and another apart from it. In history they are components in historic causes and effects, and in a causal process which links the causes with their effects. Outside history they have careers of their own, and enter into other contexts such as that of common sense, law, Existence, and so on. Inside history they are altered by one another; outside history they are realities which are the sources of the power and the being of history. When then one refers to heroes or great men in history one is either referring to an abstracted component of a genuine historic cause, or to a nonhistoric source of aberrant behavior. This means that great men are nonnatural if historic, and nonhistoric if natural. The great-man theory of history (or nationalistic theories, and the like), erroneously suppose the great man (or nation) is at once a substance in nature and an historic cause.

In history an individual is a component in a single unified cause, which also contains social or institutionalized groups as well as energy derived from nature. The individual quantizes the energy of nature and provides units for the groups. Nature makes the individuals into agents, and the groups into reservoirs of energy. The groups in turn give the individuals roles, and give nature the status of a background. The combination exhibits a controlled power over an historic space and time, in which individuals are made into coordinated contemporaries, groups become vital areas, and nature functions as a perpetual source of possible historic presents.

Were there no individuals in history, nature would exhibit energy, but there would be no causality in quantified form, and no members of historic groups. Were there no energy expended in history, individuals would be active but would not be historic agents, while groups would be impotent. Were there no groups, nature and individuals would lack historic roles and status. Historic energy is displayed only so far as there has been a synthesis of individuals, nature, and groups; and this synthesis in turn requires that these have a reality outside history. Though autonomous, history is carried by nonhistoric beings; by coming into history those beings acquire new functions and meaning.

Men are in history only so far as they interplay with nature. That nature is continuous with raw, cosmic Existence. Did men deal with that raw Existence rather than with the limited pertinent part of it that is nature, they would have to struggle with the entire cosmos at every moment. Did men deal only with a fragment of that raw Existence as caught within some limited objects in the environment, they would be social and political beings, but not necessarily historic ones. To cut nature off from Existence, as one does in society or the state, is to have it too humanized; to cut nature off from history is to leave it too unhumanized.

Nature is, with man, a constituent of history; like

man it has a being outside history as well. Having attained the stage where he had become a public being interlocked with other public beings to constitute a society or political unit, a man can become an historic being, provided that a part of Existence is already pertinent to him. Precisely because nature is no more and no less ready than man to constitute a distinctive region with him, it must possess a potentiality to be part of history.

Men are historic beings so far as they are united with an independent nature. That nature is not used by them—for that is the work of technology and economics—but is rather a coordinate factor, a power interacted with and transformed to yield a new reality. The men, of course, apart from the nature with which they interplay, have some of nature's existence within them; otherwise they could do nothing. Nature, on the other hand, is already germane to the men; otherwise men would be faced with one undifferentiated alien cosmos.

Both men and nature gain by becoming part of the historic world. Men get a satisfaction of some of their needs from history, but not a completion of themselves as individuals; nature also benefits there from the contribution mankind makes to it, but continues nevertheless to be independent and powerful, often ominous and sometimes benign. Both can exist outside of history, where of course they do not enjoy the benefits they otherwise would derive.

The historic world does not neatly balance the contributions of men and nature. It is biased towards public men; it is they which make the juncture of themselves and nature an historic reality. Had there been a bias towards nature, the result would have been a distinctive temporal ahistorical process— evolution, for example. Evolution is not historic; it is a correlative of the historic, matching history's stress towards man with one of its own towards nature.

Historic men are members of one persistent, accumulative mankind; they acquired that position through the help of nature. The combination of public men with a nature still outside the human realm has a power and a being of its own only so far as the men and nature sustain it. Nevertheless, it is a genuine product, truly present.

The historic present passes away. When it does men lose contact with the vitality of the nature in which they had shared, thereby becoming historically past, static, factual, while the energy they themselves possess is pulled along by nature as it moves on into the future. At every moment men must therefore make an effort to maintain control of some existence in order to remain in the present, and must continue to interplay with nature in order to be able to act in history. The passing away of the present historic moment thus involves a passing away of nature and men as concrete dynamic historic present beings. But men and nature, since they have a being outside the historic, are able to continue to be and to come together again to constitute still other historic unities.

Every historic occurrence is concrete, unique, actual here and now. Predictions are pre-dictions, savings in advance, put in general terms. No historic occurrence can therefore be predicted in its full concreteness. Also, the activity of men and of nature are charged with spontaneity. Both act from within and, even where law-abiding, express themselves freshly on each occasion. But even if both their activities were rigidly determined, and even if the course of their interaction were completely prescribed in advance, the actual interplay of the two would be an occurrence which took place in ways beyond the grasp and control of any general, universal form. Universals are repeatable, duplicable, nontemporal in nature and cannot entirely encompass the unique, time-bound, substantial, and active occurrences of history.

The juncture of men and nature is not necessary. Their product need not have been. It is something newly made, beyond the reach of a complete prediction. But though it is the case that each product is a contingent and unpredictable, it is possible to treat it as necessitated inside history. Each occurrence can be related to predecessors and successors through the agency of laws, purposes, structures and the like.

An occurrence, once past, is without power to act. It is a pure phenomenon, all surface, merely what it presents itself to be. It is just a fact, no longer possessing existence within it continuous with an existence outside it. A fact, to be sure, is a kind of form, but it is one which is particularized, nongeneral. This is in part because it is integral to an entire series of facts, from which it can be separated only by losing its place in a singular series of occurrences, and in part because it has a determinateness which reveals its dependence on a departed existence in a succeeding present, to which it necessarily points as the agency precluding it from being repeatable.

Since Aristotle took a rather dim view of history, it has rarely been noted how appropriate some of his distinctions are to history. The preceding and following discussion provides a new meaning and gives new application to some of those distinctions, though this was not one of its aims.

In order to explain the complex realities about him, Aristotle found it desirable to distinguish four factors or "becauses." The development of a mathematical science with a mechanical bent unfortunately led to their rather precipitate abandonment. From the time of Descartes on, only one of Aristotle's "becauses" has been taken seriously by most thinkers; it alone has been termed a "cause." Most moderns deal only with an "efficient cause," an antecedent which in time is replaced by its effect. Aristotle not only refused to exclude other types of "cause" but understood "efficient cause" to operate in a way not acknowledged in most of the later accounts. His "efficient cause" is an accumulated effective "because" or reason, not the "efficient cause" in the past of modern science. Thus in his explanation of the movement of projectiles he speaks of what had been as that which continues to operate, as that which adds to what it had begun to effect. In living beings and in the psyche, an "efficient cause" was, for him, an accumulated power or meaning making itself felt in a present. It is conceivable that one need not have recourse to an accumulated past to account for mechanical motions. But can it be avoided when we seek to understand biologic growth, psychological disturbances, political traditions, and the course of history? History makes use of something like an Aristotelian efficient cause.

Somewhat correlative to Aristotle's "efficient because" is a "final because," the end which governs a course of activity. Aristotle at times spoke as though there were definite places in the universe which exerted a final causal action on bodies, forcing them to move to those places. A better account of gravitation, making no reference to final causes, mathematical in form and universal in application, is one of the great achievements of modern science. But a reference to a final cause is needed if we are to explain the directed course of evolution, the growth of particular beings, and the course of history. A kitten becomes a cat, even though one reads to it, feeds it, and houses it as though it were a child, in part because its future continually reassesses what it is and does. And what is true of the kitten is true of mankind as it inches forward in history.

A "final because" is a discriminatory cause, having a different task at every moment. An Aristotelian "formal because," in contrast, determines the profile of what is to be; it prescribes in advance the area in which occurrences will take place. Aristotle's way of putting it is to say that actuality precedes potentiality, that the kitten is not only reorganized at every moment by the reassessing final end for it, but that it is initially and persistently governed by an excellence which it seeks to accommodate. The historic ideal, as will be soon evident, functions as a formal as well as a final because, at once directing and measuring the value of the past.

A "material because" is somewhat correlative to a "formal because." Its nature unfortunately is not made very clear by Aristotle. He usually treats it as though it were somehow inferior in being, meaning and explanatory power to the others, and frequently as though it were nothing more than a description of the stuff to be found in a being. But it is in fact close to, perhaps even identifiable with what subsequent thought took to be a stretch of "efficient causes"—an irreducible foundation, spatially extended and lasting over a period of time, to which various occurrences are to be referred for explanation and occasion. An historic "material because" is an extended stretch of items in a sequence, in which the earlier items are related as causally significant, i.e., as necessitating what follows. Treated as the correlative of the formal because, the material because will include the entire past as necessarily terminating in but not necessarily producing the present. The modern efficient cause is an analytic element, a subdivision of such a material because, a unit in a patterned sequence terminating in the present.

The relation between an occurrence and its successor has sometimes been said to be the product of a habit, of a mind, or of a time. The last is closer to reflecting the meaning of the relations holding between predecessors and successors in objective history. But the time is then to be thought of as essentially uniting rather than as separating the earlier and the later. The historic world is "organic." Here "organic" has a meaning similar to that given to it not only by Aristotle but by common sense and naturalists. For them it refers primarily to a structured being in which we can distinguish a sequence of occurrences having accumulative significance, and subject to constant reassessment by an end. This does not mean that the historic world is alive, that it has a mind, intentions, purposes, instincts and the like, but only that it cannot be understood without taking account of aspects of reality which have been more or less neglected because irrelevant to the formal mastery of nonhistorical and nonorganic beings.

9

The Accumulated Past

AN HISTORIC OCCURRENCE is the product of the
juncture of mankind and nature, with a stress on the
role of man. It is more in consonance with our usual
mode of discourse, however, to term such a world
historic only so far as it is known or can be known by
historians. If we keep to this usual way of speaking
we will tend, I think, to ignore the fact that objective
history presupposes action by the Ideal and by God.
But without the first there is no way of explaining
satisfactorily the historicity and encounterability of
the past, and without the second, no way of account-
ing for the externality and severability of that past. If
the past is not historic, not encounterable, not external, and not severable, what is it which the historian seeks to know? what is it that took place before
he came on the scene? how can he check his inferences? how can what has been have any bearing
at all on what is to be? why should the past then

not prove to be a serious overwhelming burden?

Despite the fact that not every past occurrence is causally significant for the historic present, and despite the fact that one present gives way to another, each present provides a perspective in terms of which all the past, the causally significant as well as the causally insignificant, continues to be historic. This the historic present can do, for it is at once rooted in the present of nature, and serves to orient an historic ought-to-be. Though an historian might prefer to use some one moment as his starting point and might be content to refer only to the past of what he there observes, his preferred item and its past do not in fact have an historic status denied to what he pushes aside. His preferred item is of course relevant to certain past items and is to be preferred if he is interested in those items. But his preferences do not affect the being or the course of history.

Were causally insignificant items, i.e., those past items which did not contribute to the nature or being of the present, without historic status, part of the past would cease to be united with the past on which the historian focuses, or all of the past, the causally significant as well as the causally insignificant, would be part of nature. In the latter case, nature would be a source not only of possible historic presents, but of the past to which an historian might attend. The past would then be a potentiality in nature awaiting the historian's isolation of it by means of a perspective taken from the position of the present. But the past is objectively determinate, and what is determinate is never reducible to the potential. The historian may construct a past, but he tries and ought to make it match a past which is fixed, rigid, fully determinate, never to be altered or undone. And that past includes what is and what is not significant for the occurrences in which he is interested. The past in which the historian is not interested is as real, as determinate, as historic as the part in which he is interested.

When the historian speaks of some future moment, or of the final outcome of history, he but anticipates the way in which nature, through the help of man, is realized in the guise of an historic present. When he attends only to the causally significant he in effect divorces the potentiality of future presents *for* history (contained in the reference of the human realm, nature and the Ideal to one another as capable of being conjoined) from a present *of* history (produced through the actual juncture of the human realm, nature and the Ideal). But causally insignificant past occurrences, though they do not directly contribute to the present, are on a footing with those past occurrences which do. All of the past is a past for whatever historic present there be. Every historic present consequently has an historic past which in part may be causally significant and in part causally insignificant. The historic present is a present pertinent to all that takes place in historic time; it is richer than any causally produced present need be.

But what can make the causally insignificant past part of the historic world? The causally significant cannot make the causally insignificant historic; it excludes the insignificant. Nature does not make it historic; instead it provides it with a locus. We must acknowledge a prescriptive power, an effective demand that what is not causally significant be part of history. Can anything other than an Ideal make such a demand?

There is warrant for concluding from a consideration of ethics that there is an absolute Ideal, an obligating end in terms of which men ought to act. Were there no such Ideal, there would be nothing, apart from the fiat of some authority—other men, societies, law or God—which would serve to measure both useful and useless acts as good or bad. Even some such goal as pleasure, or the good of all mankind, can be justified only if it measures up to the demands of what ought-to-be. This ought-to-be is an ethically significant absolute, having pertinence to whatever men may do at any time; it is, I have elsewhere argued, cosmic in scope, though obligating only men.

Since the historic world encompasses but part of the cosmos, and since it embraces only some of the public and nothing of the private side of man, the absolute Ideal, if it is to be pertinent to history, must be limited in range. Only an historic ideal, which is a specialization of an effective absolute Ideal, can be efficacious in history. Unlike the absolute Ideal, which might forever be unsatisfied by what men, severally and together and over all time, might do, that historic ideal is an ought-to-be that must be realized in time. What it loses in range it makes up in efficacy.

The historic ought-to-be, since it is relevant to presents yet to come, cannot be identified with any present that has already been attained. In and of itself it is a possibility pertinent to all that occurs, has occurred, and will occur in historic time. An occurrence, now taking place, faces a limited relevant form of that possibility in the guise of a projected outcome; the projected outcome in turn defines a limited number of preceding items to be part of the present occurrence (see p. 145). The projected outcome is the historic ideal qualified by the tendencies of a present occurrence; apart from that projected outcome there would be no genuine units in history, no true periods, no climaxes. It is the neglect of this role of the ideal that has made it possible for some to maintain that objective history is one undifferentiated stretch, to be organized, structured, and given meaning by the historian. But the historic past evidently has an organization, structure, and meaning of its own, with peaks and valleys; an historian makes justified divisions by attending to it.

The historic ideal is mediated by projections from the present, and thereby is able to determine the relevance of some past items to that present. The ideal is also oriented by the present towards the past, and thereby given the opportunity to add the *entire* past to the present so as to constitute one historic realm. This the ideal does by evaluating the present and thereby all that does and all that does not contribute to that present.

The historic ideal is an historic ought-to-be, in terms of which whatever has been and is now happening has a value in history. For that ought-to-be there is no difference except in value between one past fact and another. Each is measured, evaluated, hierarchically ordered by it without disturbing its place in a serial order.

If we accept something here and now to be real, the past, to which the ought-to-be gives an historic role, will also have to be found here and now. And this we have already seen is the case (see p. 85 ff.). The ought-to-be gives the past a role inside the present as an encounterable power of self-distinction, self-maintenance, directionality and self-containedness. But unless, as we shall see is the case in the next chapter, there is also some being, other than the ideal, capable of endowing the past with power sufficient to enable it to exclude and to be excluded by the present, the past will not also be external to the present, and there would consequently be nothing genuinely past to which the historians could refer when speaking of the departed past.

The historic ought-to-be, through the mediation of the present, makes all of the past historic. As standing outside the past, it offers a standard of excellence governing all that occurs. That standard can be specified to make it pertinent only to some items. Four specifications are worth distinguishing.

Firstly, the historic ideal can be dealt with as a norm which is exhausted in a given time. We look to such a norm when we try to evaluate the different members of an epoch as being more or less in gear with the spirit of a time. It is referred to when we say that we ought not to judge occurrences in an epoch except in terms appropriate to that epoch. An historian who immerses himself in a given time usually attends only to the norm exhausted in that time. He sees that an epoch's norm is fully realized in the epoch, thereby precluding any criticism of the epoch. Instead of passing judgment on the Babylonians, for example, he therefore is content to say just what they did, and where.

One can also judge an epoch in terms of what comes after it. The nature of a civilization is partly expressed in the way it allows and indeed grounds the possibility of a succeeding one. When we look back at the course of history and contrast our present with the entire past we, by taking ourselves, our virtues, powers, or ways of behaving to offer a test of that past, judge the past in terms of what comes after it. Instead of immersing ourselves in other times—which would of course already show that we were able to transcend the limitations of an ordinary relativism—we here remain inside the present. Since the present is constantly changing, history, from this position, must be constantly rewritten.

A third specification of the historic ought-to-be relates to all actual and prospective history. It takes some men, society, state, people, religion, or freedom, justice and the like to be ideal cases, paradigms, models. All history it maintains is to be judged in terms of them. But which of these measures ought we to take as our standard? To answer that question we must have recourse to a fourth specification of the historic ought-to-be. This measures every portion of history. By means of it one can judge all history. In terms of it we can say that any part or even all of the past is not as good as it might have been. This fourth specification of the historic ought-to-be need never be realized. If it is not, it will not have an historic role; though it measures the historic it will remain outside the historic world.

The last two norms enable one to evaluate all of history. But they are not necessarily realized in the course of history. In this respect they differ from the historic ought-to-be, as well as from the first two measures of excellence. Like the last two, the historic ought-to-be gives all occurrences a value, a rationale and a direction. But unlike any of them—unless it be the fourth—it operates whether or not men judge the past in terms of it.

Most of us, though, know of the historic past only through the work of the historian. The guise and meaning the past has for and through us on the future is determined in part by what we learn about the past from him. He does not thereby enable the past to be preserved. The historic past is preserved in the historic present, regardless of what men know or do.

Historians take it for granted that they know the present, and that they have a technique for knowing the past. And it seems clear that they do know something of the present, for like the rest of us, they are at home in the familiar common-sense world of everyday. But they do not encompass the whole of the present; they do not know it with full objectivity, free from bias, prejudgment, distortion and error. Still, they know it on the whole, and in principle can eliminate every subjective and extraneous element in it. And though the past is gone, never to be encountered in *propria persona*, it too can be known, and even (as we saw) encountered. Some historians believe that by induction and extrapolation they also can know what the future will be. They do of course occasionally make shrewd predictions; their expectations and anticipations are not always betrayed. But no one of them knows with surety exactly what will ensue. Nor does any one else.

The historian has no way of standing outside the agencies by means of which he studies and understands history. He therefore can provide no test of the truth of his judgments. But as a man he knows, as we know, that what he says might be true or might be false, that he might be prejudiced, narrow, out of gear with the facts. He knows that despite the fact that as an historian he cannot know the historic world as it stands outside and over against recorded history, he and we can know it in another way. That is why it is possible to speak about the historic ought-to-be, and of the need to pay some attention to the existence of obstacles in the way of the effective course of the historic world.

The ought-to-be for history operates without human guidance or supervision, through the present, thereby making what has been into a past for that present. It is hard to determine what it demands. It seems to me it can do no more or less than demand that all men live in consonance and fulfill their promise, severally and together, and that they together pursue the arts and technology, commerce and the sciences in peace and prosperity. But whatever it demands, it evaluates the present as more or less adequate, as more or less desirable, as falling short to some extent of what ought to be. Such an evaluation permits of an evaluation of all the past, the causally insignificant no less than the causally significant. So far as the present is less than it ought to be, what is causally significant for it will be evaluated as undesirable, and what is causally insignificant for it as desirable; so far as the present is as it ought to be these values of the causally significant and insignificant will be reversed. This is possible because both are caught within the perspective of the historic ought-to-be.

The historic ought-to-be comes into being when men enable the absolute Ideal to act on themselves as united with nature. The Ideal, through the mediation of men, turns a present in nature into an historic present by defining whatever precedes nature's present to be a desirable or undesirable past. At every moment the ought-to-be relates all the past, the causally insignificant as well as the significant, to the historic present, to make the present at once an outcome of the causally significant and the last term of a sequence of causally insignificants, both lines assessed as more or less desirable.

For the historian there is nothing of more importance than a present outcome and the past which is causally significant for it. He attends only to part of the past and interprets the rest in the light of what he focuses on. He does not then necessarily falsify what in fact occurs. Having rightly taken his stand with an achieved present he deals only with what is causally significant for it. But it would be wrong for him to deny the historic reality of whatever in the past is not in direct line with his accepted present content. The causally insignificant past is as historic as the significant.

There are warmongers today, as I suppose there always have been. Because it is so easy to forget that children are blinded and crippled, that starvation, disease, fanaticism, and meaningless destruction are inseparable from the conduct of even the most nobly inspired war, men readily overstate themselves in times of stress and urge acts of violence which, on reflection, they would have opposed. Be that as it may, if the warmongers are productive of historic effects they are part of a causal line which terminates in the war they help promote. If they are not effective they are causally insignificant and would not normally interest the historian. But they would nevertheless have the historic role of obstacles in the way of the achievement of the peace that prevailed instead.

Were a present held apart from the historic ought-to-be it would offer a perspective on whatever was causally significant for it. It could then itself function as an historic ought-to-be, but one which was relevant only to what was effective for it. Yet what is causally relevant to the present may not only be undesirable but may contribute to some later undesirable present; what is not causally relevant to that present may be desirable and may even have a bearing on a subsequent desirable present. The fact that the irrelevant part of the past was produced by the very agencies which brought about the relevant part shows that the irrelevant part should not be treated as though it were nonhistoric. It is a genuine part of the historic past, and ought to be seen to have a place in history, contributing to the being and presence (even though it does not act as a cause) of it.

The historic ought-to-be is operative in history. It brings what is outside the perspective of the present into relation with that present. By turning the irrelevant past into a desirable or undesirable restraint on the process by which that present came to be it enables that past to contribute to the being of the present. Because of the historic ought-to-be, the insignificant past has the role of a cross grain, of a conditioning medium which modified the pace of historic causation.

Both those who follow a life of action and those who adopt an attitude which they think is in consonance with the final upshot of history are historically oriented men, but neither does justice to the role of the historic ought-to-be. Both of them abstract from the single state of affairs which embraces all that occurs in history, the one ignoring all that is causally insignificant, the other all that is not endorsed by the supposed final outcome. Each, in a different way, consequently fails to make provision for some parts of the past.

The man of action does not know whether or not his life and work will play a significant role in the future. But even if what he did remained significant forever after, he would not have made provision for what in the past did not, directly or indirectly, produce what in fact ensued. Not all that the historic ought-to-be defines to be in the historic past is part of the historic past for him. On the other hand, he who views all occurrences in the light of an historic ought-to-be not oriented in an actual present, does not know whether or not that ought-to-be will eventually be realized. He is therefore unable to make provision for actual occurrences which are not in consonance with the ought-to-be. His attitude precludes an historic role for what in terms of the historic ought-to-be is undesirable. But history contains both the desirable and the undesirable.

We need not side with men who attend only to effects or only to the historic ought-to-be. We can avoid these extremes by recognizing that the historic ideal operates through the present to encompass whatever has happened to public men in interaction with one another and a nature beyond. Some of the past occurrences that ideal will evaluate as being desirable, while others it will evaluate as being undesirable. Desirable causes will be those which promote a present in consonance with the ought-to-be; undesirable obstacles will be those which do not promote such a present.

The best of historic-minded men are those who assume an attitude in accord with the historic ought-to-be and work to bring about what promotes its eventual realization. We choose properly when we accept good present outcomes as well as the ought-to-be, the former orienting the latter, the latter evaluating the former and whatever precedes it. We will then function as desirable causes of later presents so far as those presents are evaluated by the ought-to-be as desirable, and we will have the role of desirable obstacles for later presents which are evaluated by the ought-to-be as not being desirable. All that happened in the past will in fact and for us be relevant to ourselves and our desirable presents, either in the form of desirable causes or undesirable obstacles.

However, it is to be noted that we can work on behalf of a harmony of present outcomes and the ought-to-be in two distinct ways. To be effective historic men, living in consonance with the historic ideal, each of us must choose one of two equally valid types of historic life. We must choose between a life, as soldiers say, "in the service" (of mankind), and a contemplative one. Which is to be preferred? According to the *Bhagavad Gita* (which seems here to be in accord with the practices of the Catholic Church and the attitude of democracies) both lives are equally good. The *Gita* adds that this is true only if the man of service detaches himself from the fruits of his efforts. In effect it thus says that a life of service is satisfactory if the individual separates himself off from the stream of events of which his service is a part. Such an answer is actually biased towards the contemplative dimension. That bias should be compensated by another.

The contemplative man should recognize that his life also has consequences. These flow from the very fact that he is a man who inescapably interacts with other men, with groups, and eventually with nature. Those consequences are external to his private being, making him an historically oriented contemplative. Since they are added on as it were from the outside, he is in the same position as the man of service who detaches himself from his fruits. As the *Bhagavad Gita* seems to affirm (but which it does not and cannot show, in the light of the bias it has towards religion), the two lives can evidently not only be on a footing but can be exactly alike in value, if only the contemplative will detach himself from the achievements of his contemplation and be accredited with all the fruits of the man of action, and if the man of action, who has detached himself from his fruits, is accredited with all the achievements of the contemplative.

There is of course a difference between the two kinds of historic men, not only in the way they begin but in what they do with respect to the effects to which they are externally related. The man of service produces fruits which are accredited to the contemplative; the contemplative achieves spiritual values which are accredited to the man of service. A man is wise to choose either type of life, if he wishes to benefit from history. But both kinds are needed, the first in order that things be brought under better control, the second in order that the good life be exemplified. A good society makes provision for both. If it has only men of service it has all men function as means to values, postponing the day when their actions will be justified. If it has only contemplatives it has all primarily concerned with ends, and will make inadequate provision for their prosperity or continuance. Both lives, when properly filled out, are equal in value, but a society needs both because they are correlative.

Most societies wobble uncertainly from a stress on one of these lives to a stress on the other. While India is slowly becoming aware of its great need for men of service, China has already shifted its emphasis to make itself essentially a society of such men, and we can reasonably expect a movement there in the opposite direction one of these days. Americans, on the other hand, are apparently becoming more and more aware that the contemplative life is not only worth living but is necessary if there is to be a good society, while Ceylon continues to stress the value of the contemplative life, leading one to expect a subsequent movement in the opposite direction in the not too distant future. A caste or aristocratic society not only tries to encourage both types of life at the same time, but allocates them to different strata. In the end this seems to mean that men of service are made into servants of the men of contemplation. In a good society, the lives would be made fully co-ordinate and be mutually beneficial.

A complete life requires the realization of the absolute Ideal, and not only of the historic ought-to-be which the two kinds of lives, in correlative ways, are engaged in realizing. The exterior fruits which are accredited to the contemplative must include whatever there is, and then only so far as it has been harmonized and enriched by being subjected to the demands of the absolute Ideal. And since a complete life requires the fulfillment of a man's entire promise, the detachment which is required of the man of service must permit him to recover himself as a being existing not only outside the historic world but as one who lives fully in the light of whatever nonhistoric realities there be. The good life is one in which the nonhistoric private side of a contemplative man is supplemented by an ideally perfected world; or equivalently, in which the public life of a man of service is supplemented by a full private life, geared to all that is real.

The historic ideal enables the present to encompass what had been; it is because of it therefore that we can rightly speak of the next world war as the third of three. The next world war can be the third world war only because the previous wars can be objectively added to make the next war be a third. That war is objectively third only so far as it is related to two preceding wars. Only if they are not altogether gone can they make it a third—not to speak of the fact that the quality and flavor of that third world war will be affected by the quality and flavor of the preceding wars. To be sure, the previous wars do not arouse themselves, move out of the past and enter bodily into the third world war. If there were no traditions, no memory, no present encounters with the previous wars, the third world war would not, when present, be known as the third, and would not therefore be affected by the knowledge that the world was getting into quite bad habits. But whether one knew it or not, it would still be the case that the war was the third of three, and this not only because the previous wars had produced changes in the terrain, the methods, the objectives, and the outcomes of the subsequent war, but because the causally significant past forms a part of the very being of the present, offering it a kind of base on which to build.

The past affects the present. It also affects the future. What can be in that future is in part conditioned by what happened in the past. Had there been a destruction of all machines in the past, there would of course be no possibility of their use later. What can follow on the present is thus evidently partly determined by what the past allows to be in the future. The past helps determine what is possible in the present, and indirectly partly determines what can succeed that present.

Every past moment is determinate. Each has a successor. If that successor is past it too is therefore determinate. But a past moment faced its successor not as that which is in the past but as a possibility which was to be made determinate in the course of some present activity. The possibility once faced by a now past item had been realized as a determinate successor of that past item. The possibility has now the role only of an abstractable element in the successor.

Since the present is related to a relevant projected future, and since the present changes and therefore must face a new possibility at every moment, the terms in which the past is to be understood must be different too. The past grows larger moment by moment; some of its items necessarily achieve a new import by virtue of their new positions in larger wholes. All of the past must as a consequence be constantly reassessed.

The historic ought-to-be is definitory of the range of past history, and it provides that past with a measure of value. Apart from all present and past occurrences, it can offer only a sheer form, a place in which past occurrences are to be historicized. Because the historic ought-to-be operates via the present it provides the present with a pertinent past. The being and meaning of that ought-to-be is realized in history. It is inescapable in the sense that once men interplay with nature, it defines what precedes the historic present to be desirable or undesirable, whether it be causally significant or not.

Philosophical historians tend to suppose that the historic ought-to-be is some desirable public condition, such as political freedom for all (Hegel), an economic situation (Marx), or a political organization (Dewey). The utopians are usually more judicious than the philosophical historians; they do not, as the philosophical historians do, confound the ought-to-be with what seems to be a desirable development, nor do they overlook the fact that the ideal condition of man embraces more than the political or economic.

The philosophical historians not only make the historic ought-to-be too often take the guise of some politically desirable outcome, but they make the mistake of supposing that it alone is effective, thereby overlooking much that is causally significant. By treating the historic ought-to-be as a specific, powerful outcome at which history is forced to arrive, they are led to ignore events which do not conform to its standard, but which may in fact have been most effective in bringing about what in fact does ensue.

As a consequence philosophical historians are unable to take account of all the elements that must be acknowledged if history is to be adequately dealt with.

The most desirable terminus of all history is now only a possibility, indeterminate in good part. Both the utopians and the philosophical historians over-determine that possibility, give it more details than it has. Where the philosophical historian specializes it by projecting into it material dredged out of the past, the utopian imagines details which are extraneous to it. The details both provide may not be— and may in fact be incapable of being—produced in the course of time.

The historian, since he inquires into the past from the standpoint of the present, inevitably assumes the posture of those who look at all things teleologically, reading the future back into the past. Were it not for his awareness that there is an historic world apart from history, he would be tempted to make history be a privately produced account having no counterpart in fact. At the very least, he takes the present as that which ought to be explained, and so far, as casting a shadow of necessity on what had gone before. He need not put any stress on the ought-to-be; he can take the present to be value-free. But because the past is a past for the present, in terms of which it has an historic role, he cannot avoid dealing with the present as that which enables the past to be available, despite the fact that it has passed away. The historian thus does for a limited portion of the past, in a written history, what the historic ideal, through the help of the present, does for all the past, and apart from all knowing.

The historic present is on-going and extended, terminating a past and projecting a future. The historic future governs a limited number of preceding occurrences, and as an ought-to-be measures all that is and has been. The historic past is a power in the present and a fact external to that present. These features can be discerned not only in history but in works of art. The second part of a symphony, now taking place in an extended present, terminates the first part of the symphony and moves towards its own characteristic terminus. The third part of the symphony, that is yet to be played, defines the limits of a present within which the second part is now a not altogether determinate occurrence. And every part of the symphony is measured by the way it illustrates and promotes an ideal beauty which the symphony ought to realize. The first part of the symphony is now operative in the second at the same time that it remains outside it as a departed fact. Looking at the second part of the symphony from the standpoint of its prospective future, we can say of it (as we can say of an occurrence in history) that it has a distinctive rationale, a law-abidingness, enabling it to be rationally related to what comes after. This does not mean that there can be no spontaneities or novelties in the course of its progression to the future, for in that progression prospects are freely actualized.

Despite these similarities, the time of history and the time of music are distinct in nature and being. They have different paces, measures, localizations, components, contents, and spaces, and are sustained by different powers. Also, we desire not only to live in history but to know it through disciplined inquiry, whereas we want only to participate in or enjoy what is here and now being played, and not to study it—though of course the music can be made the topic of another enterprise. But perhaps of equal importance is the fact that in music and in other arts we are concerned with *sharing* in what has been created by individuals, whereas in history we want to *know* what mankind has already achieved.

The historic is the cosmos limited and qualified. It has a distinctive reality, rationality, and value, achieved through a juncture of nature and the human realm. It is a world with its own characteristic space, time, and causation, each with its own units, divisions, rhythms, nature, and power. Most of it has already passed away. How then can we claim to speak truly of it, unless it somehow is kept in being not only inside but outside the present? The historic ideal enables the past to be preserved in the present, but, as we shall now see, God alone enables it also to be preserved outside that present.

The Exteriority of the Past

THROUGH THE AGENCY of the historic ideal, the past is
evaluated, and what is causally significant for the
present is thereby preserved, accumulated, carried
into the being of the present. When we attend to the
present we consequently see not merely something
which is here and now, but something sustained by
what had been, and which enables us to obtain evidence of what is no longer. But to say that the present
is now sustained by the past, or that the present
provides evidence for the past, and this by virtue of
the presence of the past within it, only points up the
fact that the past has another role as well. The past is
not only preserved in the present, it is preserved
outside the present. It is not only accumulated in the
present, but is excluded by and excludes it. But if the
past has passed away, how is it possible for it to have
reality enough to enable it to be excluded? And what
relation does the past as excluded by the present have

to itself preserved in and sustaining the present?

The departed past, it has already been noted, is not ingredient in nature; it is not a present which has become converted into a natural potentiality after it has enjoyed a moment of distinction over against the rest of nature. The past is determinate, through and through; but potentialities are indeterminate. Shakespeare is past at a definite time and place, with exactly the same number of hairs that he once had; the shape, look, weight he exhibited at a certain moment in time is what he forever possesses as at that time. Of course he is not a substantial dynamic human being any longer. As in the past, he lacks something which he possessed when the Elizabethan Age was present. Then he was existent, alive, vital, crowding out room, enduring through time, effectively acting on other things to change the course of the world. That present became past by yielding up its existence to a succeeding present.

The historic past is a series of determinate presents, denied power, effectiveness; it is without promise, without control, a mere sequence of facts. It is no historian's creation, but that to which his history must look for confirmation. But how could anything without power, which has already been pushed aside by what is here and now, have any being at all? It can evidently have no being of its own, unless in one and the same place there can be all the substantial beings which had once occupied that place, or unless somehow stretching behind us is a genuine reality which effectively excludes us as we exclude it. The first of these alternatives cannot be maintained, for it converts the past into a present. Only the second is left to us. The past stands apart from the present as a distinct abstract and settled reality. It is distinct from the present because excluded by present fact; it is abstract because it lacks the existence characteristic of actualities; and it is settled because it is determinate.

Each moment in the past excludes and is excluded by other past moments. The exclusion of the past moments one from the other does not, however, make them be in a relation of earlier and later to one another. The moments of the past and their diverse contents are in an order of before and after in and of themselves; they are earlier and later only as being further or nearer the present.

Not only do past moments exclude one another; the entire past is excluded by the present. And that past is sufficiently determinate to exclude the present in return. The exclusion of the past by the present is a function of the present's power to be an effective becoming. The exclusion of the present by the past is a function of the determinateness characteristic of the items the past contains.

The past is fully determinate, to which nothing can be added and from which nothing can be subtracted. But what is determinate must have some being. Yet the past is no substance. It is a tissue of facts. These facts are not inside the present, somehow overlaid by opposed subsequent facts. Were that the case, the present would be subdivided into countless subordinate and antagonistic facts. Nor is the past a fresh creation, forged by thought out of present actualities, for the past is not dependent for its being on the minds of men.

The past not only has a being over against the present but a being over against knowledge. Since it not only excludes but is excluded by the present and yet has no substantiality of its own, it must obtain support. It cannot get this from the future, for the future is indeterminate and cannot provide adequate support for what is determinate. Nor can the past achieve objective being through the acts of men, for their acts presuppose a settled unalterable set of determinate items which are in part constituted by a nature existing apart from men.

There is no causality in the past, no becoming; there are no substances there, no actions. But for all that it is a realm to which the historian refers when he speaks of causality, becoming, substances, and actions. The historian is not merely interested in recording, restating, inquiring into or knowing that past; he records, restates, inquiries into or knows in part in order to obtain data which he can quicken. His account can never be altogether reduced to a restatement of what the past is like inside the present; it requires that the past be exterior to the present, a source of data to be reached by inference and vitalized in a narrative.

The past has a being of its own as a fact pushed aside, repulsed by present fact. But what then sustains, what supports it? Whitehead and Hartshorne boldly answer—and I think correctly—"God." To avoid affirming that God keeps past evil in existence, however, they suppose that when God preserves the past He dislocates it from the present and adds excellence to it, or purges it of its follies. Naked, brute, unqualified evils are not on their view preserved by God. But then something occurred in the past which God does not preserve. I think what they say is true of what is in God; it is not true of what is outside Him and which He also preserves.

Everything has some modicum of evil in it. If God could not embrace past evils without adding to or altering them, He would in effect not preserve them. What God does preserve is, even on the Whitehead-Hartshorne theory, preserved by Him on His own terms. Subject to His transformations the preserved past might then well follow principles which need have no necessary bearing on what had been. But then the past could become pertinent to the present only through a fiat which somehow undid the transformations to which the supernatural being had subjected it.

A support for the past must not compromise the relevance of that past to the present. And it must make possible an unaltering preservation of every fact whatsoever, the bad as well as the good. God could, for example, make what happened be part of His being. If He did, He would transform and enhance what had been. But the past must still exist outside God. It must there, excluding and being excluded by the present, be fixed, unimproved, unaltered, needing God only to enable it to be. He who is anxious to hold to a theory of creation should say then that God creates not the present but the past, since He bestows on it a kind of existence which enables it to be external and in a relation of exclusion to the present.

No assertion perhaps will invoke as much distress as the claim that an adequate account of history requires a reference to a kind of creating God. Indeed no word seems intellectually so offensive today as the three letter one which ends the previous assertion. The ancient Hebrews, perhaps because they thought that a name was an integral part of the being which it named and thus made possible its use in magic, referred to God by means of an unpronounceable set of consonants. "Jehovah" and "Lord" are at best surrogates, signs, not genuine names. Other religious men think of God as primarily concerned with the saving of souls, and they find all usages of the term which refer to a being that might be concerned with something other than men and their welfare, perverse at best and worthless at least. Many theologians, aware that the concerns of God are wider in reach than man and his problems, nevertheless think that the proper use of the term "God" involves a reference to the particular practices, creeds, history or faith of some institution. There is, however, a long and respectable tradition in which the term is used to refer to a being superior to anything in this space-time world, but which is not absolutely perfect, not necessarily the creator of any substances, not necessarily concerned with man's salvation. Aristotle, Lucretius, Scheler, Whitehead are among a number of distinguished thinkers who have spoken of God in these objective, philosophical terms. It is in the spirit of their usage that it is here being claimed that the past is preserved by God, unaltered, exterior to, opposing and opposed by the present.

The past has a cosmic range. It needs a cosmic power to give it the kind of being which would enable it to oppose and be opposed by the present. Only God could endow the past with the strength to oppose the present as strongly as the present opposes it. Only He is broad enough, persistent enough, powerful enough to endow the past with sufficient existence to enable it properly to be. The past excludes and is excluded by the present, only so far as that past is related to the present by Him.

Though there is a sense in which the past continues to be in the present, and though men can project their various schemes backwards, there would be no genuine historic objectivity unless the modicum of existence, which had been made historic, is kept within the sphere of history, and unless also the incipient future was made relevant to the present. No being except God has the power to deal with the entire historic past, the whole of mankind, the whole of nature, and the prospective historic future.

God does not enable the past to be preserved in the present. That result is produced by the ideal operating through the agency of the present. Nor does He or can He give the past a present existence; that would turn the past into a present. He can give the past only a support, make it an irreducible, objective reality.

An historic moment is constituted by a juncture of men and nature. That moment passes away by breaking up into two components. One of these is the fact that occurred, the completely determinate juncture of man and nature. This is the occurrence as past. The other component of the departed present is the vital unity of the juncture. This is projected forward to help constitute the possible outcome of an ongoing present. The new historic moment comes to be through a coming together of nature and man in such a way as to exclude and be excluded by the departed factuality on one side, and to face a possible outcome on the other. Without God there would be no factuality which excludes and, as will be apparent, without Him there would be no possibility made relevant by something present. Without Him, consequently, there would be no new historic present moment.

God and the historic ideal supplement one another. Where the ideal makes what precedes relevant to what succeeds, He makes what succeeds relevant to what precedes; and where the ideal gives to the past an historic role inside the present, He endows the past with objectivity and power, so that it can exclude and be excluded by the present. In abstraction from them both, the historic present will have neither a luring nor a projected future, neither an accumulated nor an objective past.

God gives the past an existence, not by making its items stand on their own feet with a genuine existence in them—for as was remarked, this would make them all present—but by making them all possess the present existence at greater or less remove, as more or less immediate. The past is thus made exterior in the very act of making the historic present a present for that past. Where the historic ought-to-be evaluates the present and thereby gives relevance to an accumulated past, God relates an external past to the present and thereby gives relevance to the present with respect to that past.

It is the entire past that is God's concern. All that has occurred is placed by Him in an ordinal sequence so as to terminate in the present. The past, through His efforts, acquires a being of its own, contrasting with the being, activity and value of the present. Did God not make the past be, the historian could not refer to a realm in which whatever occurred was given a definitive place in an order with respect to all other occurrences. Without God we would lose the objectivity of the past. Since this in the end means losing the bearing of the present on the past, it means that there would be no past to know.

In effect God decrees that a fact, having once been a fact in history, cannot ever cease to be such a fact, inseparable from present existence. The past thus is more than an explanation for the present; it is really related to that present, for God sustains past occurrences to make them part of one single past, terminating in the present. The existence He gives them is historic existence. That existence enables the past to occupy a kind of historic space, have a position in an historic time and contribute to an historic

causality. Its historic space, to be sure, has no geo-
graphic extension, its historic time does not pass,
and its historic causality is not dynamic. They are
all abstract and dessicated because denied a present
existence. But because the past has a divinely be-
stowed existence, these dimensions are all to be accredited to the items which make up the past.

In the dissolution of the present historic moment,
nature's existence loses the qualifications imposed on
it by man, and becomes merged with cosmic existence. Were this the end of the story, not only would
there be only a momentary satisfaction given to nature by men, without any warrant for a recurrence,
but what was now occurring would not condition
what was subsequently possible. But God plays a role
with respect to future possibility somewhat similar to
what He does with respect to past factualities. When
He replaces the present conjuncture of man and
nature by a divinely sustained past fact, He im-
poses the vitality of the juncture on the historic ideal
that confronts the new present, thereby specifying
that ideal. The present consequently faces a prospective, relevant, historic possibility.

Just as God enables facts to have an existence in
the past, so He enables possibilities to be prospective
outcomes of present causes. There can be a next
historic moment brought about by an historic process
because the prospect which will be realized has already, through His help, been prepared for it. And
when He enables the present to become relevant to
the future, He of course incidentally also enables the
past of that present to become relevant to that future.

God is immanent in history in the sense that He
makes all history—the entire reach of the past,
the present, and the unlimited future—form one for-

ward moving totality. It is He who enables the present occurrence to project its vitality unity into the future, and who gives the achieved meaning of man and nature a being in the past. He does not do something in history in the sense of causing this or that to happen; He merely makes history into a single objective determinate reality facing a relevant future. His power to refer all past facts to the present moment as the locus of their vital existence, and to make the historic ideal take the form of a limited prospect, enables Him to be a factor in history.

Since Existence seems to act in rather constant ways, God's use of it to support the past will result in somewhat the same kind of totality, in being and content, as that which had been a moment before. The meaning characteristic of a prospect is also rather constant. In any case historic changes are for the most part small and sluggish. Though the past is always increasing and the future is always changing, for longish stretches they look somewhat as they had.

Were nature absolutely steady in its operation and effect, all historic causation would be the result of variations in the activity of man. Were mankind on the other hand always the same in feature and effect, all variations in history would have to be accredited to variations in the activities of nature. We make the first supposition when we wish to learn the kind of transformations which men undergo by virtue of their participation in history; we make the second supposition when we wish to find out how receptive or antagonistic nature is to man. From the perspective of God both factors always vary to some extent. Neither can be taken to be absolutely fixed; each changes and helps transform the other, as a rule unappreciably for short periods, signally over long. History is an adventure, more or less transforming the very items which contribute to its being.

Though God is immanent in history in the sense of enabling past and future to exclude and be excluded by the present, He stands over against history as eternal and fixed, as its very Other. This He can do because He allows the historic present to be constituted by men publicly interacting with forces outside them. He is needed to guarantee the reality and relevance of an historic past and future; the historic present does not need Him, except as a counterbalancing Other who will relieve the present, in part, from the burden of its accumulated past.

God could not preserve the past unless there were a past to preserve. Since the past is produced by the passing away of presents, it has new content added to it at every moment. God gives each present, as it passes away, the status of a past item capable of standing over against what preceded it and what succeeds it. Did He do only this he would in effect be pushing what had been past, further and further away from the present. He could have accomplished the same result in a single act, by making a receptacle into which all occurrences, in their passing away, inevitably flowed. But the historic is no mere sequence of items; it is more than past items, causally significant or otherwise, which terminate in an historic present. The past is an accumuaated burden from which the present must be freed. There is freedom in history because the past which is inherited is not allowed to crush the present. The act of enabling the present to act freely is one with the act of allowing that past to be outside but relevant to that present. It is thus one and the same thing to say that God frees the present from the burden of the inherited past, and that He preserves that past and its associated obstacles outside that present.

The historic present is weighed down by its inherited past. God, by lessening the load of that inheritance on the present, enables the present to have an integrity of its own. We have here an act on God's part which is similar to what, as Scheler saw, is to be accomplished by repentance. But God does not operate on all the items inherited in the present in the same way, for they do not all have the same weight. His is a differentiating act, varying in degree and kind at every moment, in consonance with the role which past items enjoy within the historic present. And since at every moment the present fails to accommodate itself fully to the release offered by the divine, it ends by recovering most of its inherited past, usually with only a slightly different weight than it had before.

Past factuality is governed by an historic ought-to-be and is divinely related to the present; the present is divinely projected into a relevant future at the same time that the historic ideal gives to the past the role of sustaining the features of present things. The historic past, consequently, is an external fact and an inward power for the present; the historic future is a measure of the value of the present and a project to be realized by that present; the features of the present are given being by the past and are evaluated in a later present.

God holds the historically achieved past apart from both man and nature, and thereby enables both to act again so as to produce a new historic moment. It is He who makes it possible for the components of the historic to fall asunder, at the same time guaranteeing that what they together had achieved will be continuous with what they together will achieve.

The historian knows nothing of God's intent; but he also knows nothing of the role that God plays in making the historic past have being, or in making possible a relevant prospective meaning—or that man and nature have supplementary historic roles. Nor does he know how the past can be objective or how the present can be momentarily free. The historian does not differ from the rest of us in his grasp of God's intent—leaving aside those who have had special dispensations and messages. It is the philosopher of history who, exploring the historic with a distinctive objective and a different method, alone comes to know what history presupposes, and thus what roles are played by God, the Ideal, natural Existence, and actual men to make a history possible.

God enables historic present beings to act freely, at the same time that the historic ideal enables the past to continue to be inherited by that present. Were God without a function in history, the historic ideal would make it possible for the past to be preserved, but the being in which it was preserved would not only have its free power to act reduced, but the past would be only a phase, a subdivision or a facet of the present. The present is active and independent precisely because God enabled it to be free from the burden of the past. On the other hand, were the ideal without a function in history, God in making the past have a being of its own would in effect make that present be only the last item in an historic sequence, inheriting nothing. The historic ideal gives the past to the present but God prevents that past from destroying the present's freedom. God gives a present to the past but the ideal prevents that present from turning the past into a derivative of that present.

The historic present is the terminus of all that went before. It is the product of a blocked and braked causality interlocked with a process of inheritance. The historian focuses on that part of the present which provides him with evidence, and attends to earlier periods so far as they follow along causal lines. So far as he has no knowledge of the bearing of God and the ideal on history, his account, no matter how accurate and comprehensive, will be incomplete. He will not know how to pace his narrative properly, for he will not know that or how the causally significant was blocked and threatened. He will not know how or why historic occurrences, though burdened by the past, are nevertheless free. Nor will he know how or why the historic future controls and is controlled by what is now occurring. And he will not, of course, be able to say how or why what he affirms of the past is true.

The historian does tell us what no one else will or can. Because he is a common-sense man, he is in a rough and ready way aware that the necessities and contingencies, the outcomes and activities, the very space, time, and causation of history are unlike those to be found in other regions. Because he is an historian he knows how to move towards and in the past more effectively and fruitfully than any one else. And because he makes persistent critical use of a distinctive method of discovery, it is to him we must look to find out what in fact occurred and why. If we listen to him we will come to understand our public selves, our common background and our possible future to a degree we otherwise could not, and as a consequence we may more readily become more fully what we ought to be.

INDEX

INDEX

Index